Praise for *Learning to Be Fair*

This marvelously balanced, penetrating, and eminently readable interdisciplinary study of "equity" deftly grapples with the historical and linguistic complexity in the use of the word, and brings much-needed light into overheated contemporary debates about how to foster equity and equality in various cultural settings. The volume would be a welcome guide and companion not just for academics and students seeking to better understand the concept, but also for administrators, policymakers and legal professionals grappling with practical questions of when and how to bend the rules and for what purpose.
—Amy Uelmen, director for mission and ministry, Georgetown University Law Center, and lecturer in religion and professional life, Georgetown University

With impressive historical knowledge and moral insight, McNamara helps us move beyond the narrow confines of procedural justice to consider questions of substantive fairness. He shows us how the venerable concept of equity can provide guidance not only for today, but also for the future of our diverse and pluralistic societies.
—Cathleen Kaveny, Libby Professor of Law and Theology, Boston College

With *Learning to Be Fair*, Charles McNamara offers timely assistance to readers at every level who are struggling to understand the roots and sources of our present-day conversations about equity in the workplace, on our campuses, and in public life. Written in an accessible way that spares no effort to explore the richness of how our civilization came to understand and value equity, McNamara's book belongs in the board room as much as the classroom. Every reader could profit from *Learning to Be Fair* as a guide to navigate these challenging conversations today—conversations McNamara assures us are as ancient as they are contemporary.
—Steven P. Millies, professor of public theology and director of the Bernardin Center, Catholic Theological Union

Learning to Be Fair

Learning to Be Fair

Equity from Classical Philosophy to Contemporary Politics

Charles McNamara

Fortress Press
Minneapolis

LEARNING TO BE FAIR
Equity from Classical Philosophy to Contemporary Politics

Copyright © 2024 Fortress Press, an imprint of 1517 Media. All rights reserved. Except for brief quotations in critical articles or reviews, no part of this book may be reproduced in any manner without prior written permission from the publisher. Email copyright@1517.media or write to Permissions, Fortress Press, PO Box 1209, Minneapolis, MN 55440-1209.

29 28 27 26 25 24   1 2 3 4 5 6 7 8 9

Library of Congress Control Number: 2024937556 (print)

Cover illustration by Ashley Muehlbauer with compilation of portrait illustrations from Getty Images: Saint Thomas Aquinas/duncan1890; Vintage engraving of a Portait of Cicero/duncan1890; and Vintage engraving of a Statue of Aristotle/duncan1890; Portrait of Alexander Hamilton/mikroman6; Plato (428/427 BC-348/347 BC), Greek philosopher, wood engraving, published 1864/ZU_09.
Cover design: Ashley Muehlbauer / A M Book Design

Print ISBN: 978-1-5064-9509-5
eBook ISBN: 978-1-5064-9510-1

Contents

Acknowledgments   vii

Introduction   1

1 The Soft, Leaden Rule   9

2 The Roman Refashioning of Equity   39

3 Revolutions in Equity   65

4 Modern Equity—Critics and Contraries   91

5 Learning to Be Fair   115

Conclusion   139

Notes   147
Bibliography   165
Index   171

Acknowledgments

This book grew out of a June 2022 essay published in *Commonweal*, a magazine for which I have written with some regularity. I am grateful to its staff for nurturing my writing, and I extend particular thanks to Matthew Boudway for his years of editorial guidance. Similarly, I thank Ryan Hemmer and the staff at Fortress Press for their expeditious work as we brought this volume to fruition.

My thinking regarding equity was also enriched in early 2023 during an extended visit to Washington and Lee University, where I was the Class of 1963 Scholar in Residence. Special gratitude goes to Tim Lubin, Howard Pickett, and the several students, faculty members, and staff who generously spent their time with me. My warmest thanks are due to my *amici carissimi* Caleb M. X. Dance and Lily van Diepen, who hosted me during this productive and stimulating residency.

Outside academic institutions and publishing houses, many friends have volunteered their attention and criticism. Among them are Frances Mitchell, Beatrice Mitchell, Paul Sperry, Laura Saunders, Dahlia Tyson, Carolyn Kormann, Elina Tetelbaum, Matthew Anderson, Nitin Ahuja, and Alan Rozenshtein. My current colleagues Steve Ahearne-Kroll and Eva von Dassow, too, have kindly encouraged my publishing endeavors.

Many former colleagues from Columbia University offered guidance as I drafted these chapters, especially Joe Sheppard, Kate Meng Brassel, Zachary Roberts, Richard John, and Claire Catenaccio. Foremost among them is Kathy Eden, whose own lucid, perceptive writing on equity stands as a scholarly exemplar. The threads that come together in this book, moreover, bear on several texts that I had the good fortune to teach in Columbia's Core Curriculum. Alongside individuals named above, dozens of fellow instructors, scores of insightful students, and the staff in the Center for the Core Curriculum all catalyzed my intellectual development for many years, and to them all I am deeply grateful. I was able to write this book efficiently—pleasurably, even—in large part due to their invaluable support.

Introduction

"It has also been asked, what need of the word 'equity'?"[1]

You yourself may have asked this question lately, spurred by the multiplication of seminars in your workplace on diversity, equity, and inclusion or perhaps by the equity-language guides proliferating at universities and even professional groups like the American Medical Association.[2] And if you have not been asking what to make of this ascendant language, then at least your neighbors have. As Google's graphs of its users' search terms make clear with steeply upward slopes, the phrase *diversity, equity, and inclusion* was practically nonexistent in queries until about 2014, ballooning in 2020 alongside the twin crises of the Covid-19 pandemic and the George Floyd protests.[3] Like new slang unfamiliar to superannuating ears, *equity* has crept into the cultural landscape, leaving the uninitiated to turn to search engines to decode the language we hear at school, work, and even home.

That apparent novelty, however, belies the long, rich history that *equity* has had in American culture, reaching far beyond the beginning of our current century. The question above—"What need of the word 'equity'?"—was not posed by today's pundit class or political aspirants, nor was it entered into Google's all-knowing search box. It was instead published in a newspaper column in June 1788, pseudonymously signed *Publius* but penned by a young activist named Alexander Hamilton. And

Hamilton's column was not asking this question to deride an ascendant notion of social justice. He instead considered whether the principle of "equity," a principle cited in centuries of English legal and political writing, had any place in the document that would become the US Constitution. As students of American history know well, Hamilton—alongside his *Federalist* coauthors, John Jay and James Madison—wrote these essays to help his fellow citizens "decide the important question, whether societies of men are really capable or not, of establishing good government from reflection and choice, or whether they are forever destined to depend, for their political constitutions, on accident and force."[4] After "reflection and choice" about the nation under which these citizens would consent to be governed, the Americans did, in fact, ratify a constitution in which the "judicial Power shall extend to all Cases, in Law and Equity."[5]

You would be forgiven for not knowing that *equity* appears in the central political conversation of early America. Despite its approving treatments in the writings of the framers and its appearance in the constitution, "equity" has mostly found itself in the crosshairs of bitter contemporary partisanship. In *National Review*, Christopher Caldwell warns that we "might call equity a no-excuses imperative to eliminate all collective racial inequalities."[6] Rather than see equity as "a new name for something that Americans have been arguing about for two or three generations"—the equal treatment of minority groups and the expansion of civil rights—Caldwell argues that "the equity movement is radically new." Christopher Rufo, perhaps best known for orchestrating the takeover of Florida's New College, presents equity in similarly alarmist language. In his view, an "equity-based form of government would mean the end not only of private property but also of individual rights, equality under the law, federalism, and freedom of speech."[7] This pernicious principle of "neo-Marxism," he adds, "is easily confused with the American principle of equality."

Criticism of the rise of "equity" also comes from the political left. The democratic-socialist magazine *Jacobin* catalogs how corporate executives institute "racial equity" seminars in the workplace, but by "requiring staffers to attend anti-racism training," Jennifer Pan finds that "the boss remains the ultimate arbiter of who's racist and who's not."[8] Pan includes "equity" alongside terminology like "privilege" and "white supremacy culture" as "radical-sounding language" that might excite progressive activists, but in her view, these terms ultimately provide cover for "employers to consolidate their power over employees under a veneer of social justice." Zeeshan Aleem recently discussed another example of this kind of corporate cynicism at the outdoor retailer Recreational Equipment Incorporated. By cloaking union-busting propaganda in the language of "the co-op's values of workplace diversity, equity and inclusion," its corporate leaders tried to signal that they are "on the right side of things and should be trusted while offering zero concessions" to employees seeking collective bargaining rights.[9] There is, then, no shortage of discontent surrounding "equity" in contemporary life. Across the political spectrum, pundits and critics increasingly see it not so much as a concept but as a cudgel.

Against this rising tide of suspicion, this book aims to rehabilitate our understanding of equity by anchoring its meaning in the rich philosophical, pedagogical, and lexicographical accounts spanning more than two thousand years that have brought this word to us today. These traditions make clear that equity is not the invention of human-resources departments nor of radical political activists. It is instead one of the most durable, central, and perplexing ideas of Western ethical and political thought. Indeed, resolving the perennial problems that equity raises—those surrounding equality, merit, and the law—is beyond the scope of this one book. The chapters that follow do not present one uncomplicated, "correct" account of what equity ought to mean today. But they do present an intellectual backdrop that can inform the often-paradoxical ways in which we think and talk about this principle. Before we ourselves ask what need there is of the word *equity* today, we would do well to understand what this foundational principle has meant and how it—even without our noticing its influence—continues to guide our intuitions about justice, fairness, and equality.

The chapters of this book proceed roughly chronologically, beginning with seminal texts of Greek philosophy that set in motion the terminology and debates that would later take root in our contemporary legal and ethical conversation. The first begins with Plato's *Republic*, in which Plato treats a question that vexes us still today: "What is justice?" Socrates, the central character of Plato's dialogue, answers this question by presenting a theory of so-called forms: immutable, abstract concepts like the good, the beautiful, and the just. As Plato's most famous student, Aristotle is well acquainted with these forms but also critical of them, and in the second half of this chapter, we observe how Aristotle presents justice not as an abstract principle removed from everyday dealings but as a matter of the scrappy world of Athenian law courts. In this legal context, Aristotle introduces the principle of *epieikeia*, the term that would become our word *equity*, which he describes as "the soft, leaden rule" that allows the law to "adapt itself to actual events" in the pursuit of justice. While Plato sees justice as an immutable and abstract concept, Aristotle positions it as a matter of particular, concrete, and even unpredictable legal procedure.

Although Plato and Aristotle introduce the debates surrounding justice and the law that first generate the principle of equity, their Greek word for it—*epieikeia*—is not the direct linguistic ancestor of our modern English terminology. Instead, our term *equity* comes from the Latin *aequitas*, a word that itself sits at the center of political upheavals of the dying Roman Republic. In the second chapter, we consider how *aequitas* introduced to the Romans some of the same intractable problems we grapple with today: the relationship between equity and equality, the perennial contest between democracy and aristocracy, and the persistent ambiguity regarding merit in a society of diverse citizens. As Julius Caesar, Cicero, and other figures of that tumultuous century discovered, such matters are never easily settled. In the end, the Romans show us the origins not just of our terminology but also of our stubborn disagreements about equality and fairness.

As part of these discussions of *aequitas*, legal justice, and democracy, Cicero introduces some principles of republican constitutional design, principles that would influence centuries of political thinkers of various countries. The third chapter focuses on those authors of the English legal tradition who would transplant Greco-Roman notions of equity into their own lexicons and courtrooms. More particularly, I trace the influence of Aristotelian *epieikeia* and Ciceronian *aequitas* on the emerging "courts of equity" in England and America. Excavating the writings of Thomas Hobbes, Lord Ellesmere of England's Court of Chancery, Alexander Hamilton, and a variety of postrevolutionary thinkers in the United States, this chapter culminates in the ratification of the US Constitution, whose Article III states that "the judicial Power shall extend to all Cases, in Law and Equity." In short, this chapter argues that the principle of equity—hardly the invention of twenty-first-century academics—arrived in American legal life through millennia-long traditions of classical political thought.

Even if *equity* appears in America's founding political documents, how—if at all—does it bear on our contemporary embrace of that word? Do these earlier histories from Plato to Hamilton give us any clarity about novel terms like "climate equity," "racial equity," and "housing equity"? In the fourth chapter, I answer these questions affirmatively, but I do not offer a simple way to decode our society's new terminology. Indeed, if America acquired its language and principles of equity from the ancient world, it also acquired those earlier traditions' problems and paradoxes. On account of the diverse accounts of equity in the first chapters—rendered primarily in Greek, Latin, and English—it should come as no surprise that our terminology is muddled and even outright inconsistent. To resolve these inconsistencies, I designate two species of equity that persist in modern culture: "equity of the exception" and "equity of the norm." Drawing on Aristotelian, Ciceronian, and Anglophone thought, I propose that our language of equity needs some clarification but that its imprecision has been inherited from the ancient intellectual bedrock on which it stands. Equity may be an old concept, but it has never been—and will never be—an easy concept.

In the final chapter, I consider how this vagueness should make us especially cautious in matters of education—what does it mean to teach a concept that has such contested and paradoxical meanings? Here I turn again to ancient Greece, but instead of looking at the philosophical differences between Plato and Aristotle, I show how their contemporary Isocrates positions equity as a central goal of Greek education. Unlike Plato and Aristotle, however, Isocrates redefines *epieikeia* to align with his own political and professional aims rather than with high-minded philosophical justice. For him, equity is a conservative "reasonableness" that demands we attend to "useful things," "important matters," and a respectable "reputation" among our fellow citizens. Isocrates, therefore, gives us a radically alternative understanding of equity, one just as old as the philosophers who begin our study here but one used to train students in the pursuit of renown, not justice. In his sweeping revision of equity around careerist priorities and political clout, Isocrates illustrates how values like equity can be defined either for us or by us. By way of conclusion, I urge readers to choose the latter option.

While this book attempts to provide one historical account of equity's role in political and legal thought, it is by no means an attempt to provide a comprehensive account. There are, indeed, notions of equity that remain entirely untouched in this volume, including matters of financial equity familiar to homeowners and investors. And even if these chapters span millennia of intellectual history and multiple languages, there are thinkers both within these traditions and without who do not appear in my brief argument. It is not my intention to present the authoritative account of an all-encompassing notion of equity; in my view, in fact, a simple, static account of this protean concept does not exist at all.

In that sense, this book interrogates rather than resolves the contemporary disagreements surrounding equity. It excavates some of the lexical archaeology of this term, in keeping with my academic training in ancient languages and political philosophy. Since I am neither a lawyer nor a pundit, I offer no closing arguments nor convention speeches. My book tries to keep questions open rather than closed, for words and concepts are often more complicated and contested (and therefore interesting) after capturing our attention for some time. I hope my readers will also come to view equity with fascination, more as an ethical paradox to contemplate than a mantra to memorize.

Chapter One

The Soft, Leaden Rule

In the first book of Plato's *Republic*, a man turns into a monster.

The menacing transformation interrupts Socrates's dialogue with his fellow Athenians at a religious festival in a nearby harbor town. Their topic of conversation is the meaning of justice, the central question of the *Republic*. Socrates and his companions propose and demolish several possible definitions—"helping friends and harming enemies" or perhaps "repaying one's debts"—but none can withstand Socrates's scrutiny. Surely, he argues, we should not return a loaned weapon to the insane. Justice, then, must be something more than simple repayment. And, he continues, "can just people use justice to make people unjust? In a word, can good people use their virtue or goodness to make people bad?"[1] So much for "harming enemies."

Socrates describes how Thrasymachus, no more than a silent bystander earlier, "coiled himself up like a wild beast about to spring" and "hurled himself at us as if to tear us to pieces."[2] Thrasymachus "roared into our midst," instantly transforming a chat among friends into Socrates's defense against a monstrous, enraged heckler. Despite his bestial characterization that more closely resembles caricature, Thrasymachus himself was a real person, one of the sophists of the rough-and-tumble intellectual culture of fifth-century Athens, in which Plato and Socrates lived. Only brief fragments of Thrasymachus's writings survive, so it can be difficult to separate the flesh-and-blood thinker from Plato's Socratic foil. But at least in Plato's account here, Thrasymachus's central—and perhaps most infamous—ethical and political belief is that "justice is nothing other than the advantage of the stronger."[3] He explains his definition more fully in the same scene: "Each type of city makes laws to its own advantage: Democracy makes democratic laws, tyranny makes tyrannical laws, and so on with the others. And they declare what they have made—what is to their own advantage—to be just for their subjects, and they punish anyone who goes against this as lawless and unjust. This, then, is what I say justice is, the same in all cities, the advantage of the established rule."[4]

Thrasymachus's argument is rife with cynicism and borne out of ethical relativism. According to this view, there is no objective or even principled moral ordering of right and wrong. Instead, people simply live under constructed and imposed ideas of "justice" that preserve social structures from above. In such a Thrasymachean worldview, there is nothing "truly" or even durably correct about the values of liberal democracy. They are "just" only insofar as they preserve the power and authority of liberal democracy's rulers. Similarly, an autocratic totalitarian state would not be an "unjust" form of government but instead would be "just" provided that the totalitarian state has impressed its own definition of justice on its subjects. Such a state would simply redefine justice to include unquestioning submission and conformity as qualities of a "just" person. Taken in a more general way, "just" people are simply good at following orders from those in power, regardless of what those orders might specifically entail.

According to Thrasymachus's topsy-turvy view of political justice, the most desirable position in a society is having the power to set those orders for and on everyone else. Such a person himself acts for his own benefit and commands everyone else to be "just"—setting rules that bind everyone else but abiding by no such rules himself. Seeing this kind of radical redefinition as the greatest and even most authentic kind of power, Thrasymachus concludes that "injustice, if it is on a large enough scale, is stronger, freer, and more masterly than justice. And, as I said from the first, justice is what is advantageous for the stronger, while injustice is profitable and advantageous for oneself."[5] Like some ancient, ruthless predecessor of Leona Helmsley, Thrasymachus thinks justice is only for the little people.

Socrates spends most of the *Republic* resisting Thrasymachus's vision of amoral, instrumental "justice." It's a difficult position to combat. Isn't it true that states set down rules that preserve order and structure? Aren't lawmakers happy to perpetuate the very norms that allowed them to ascend to the heights of power? And isn't Socrates the real sucker here, ultimately drinking hemlock under an Athenian "justice" that others foisted on him? But for the snub-nosed gadfly of the *Republic*—itself written decades after Socrates's historical death—justice cannot be something so malleable and cynical, and in the fourth book, he will set out his own definition of justice: "doing one's own work and not meddling with what isn't one's own."[6] Against Thrasymachus's justice, one subject to redefinition by actors and states powerful enough to do so, Socrates presents a justice that is stable, universal, and objective. This Socratic definition presents its own series of problems, perhaps first and foremost that it endorses a rigid social structure. His "justice" commands that those born into the role of the shoemaker should make shoes, that those born into the role of ship captains should captain ships, and that those born into the role of political philosophers should rule the just city with their philosophical gifts. Indeed, Socrates's definition of justice has earned generations of advocates and detractors, with some seeing his call for a caste of so-called philosopher-kings as a totalitarian state itself and others seeing his radical expansion of occupational opportunity as a forerunner of modern equality movements.

Rich and important though these debates may be, they are for another book. Here, we set aside these questions about *what* exactly justice is and instead focus on *how* thinkers like Socrates and Thrasymachus think we should look for its definition.[7] Thrasymachus contends that justice is a tool—a concept whose meaning we make up—whereas Socrates insists that justice is a concept whose definition we discover. Socrates sees justice as something stable and independent; Thrasymachus sees it as something malleable and contrived. This debate about how we understand justice may seem like a heady philosophical project best left to the faculty lounge. It is instead the crucial opening salvo for our historical consideration of "equity"; indeed, Socrates's argument for a rational and objective justice sets in motion all kinds of difficult and ongoing debates about politics and ethics that continue to rattle modern life as we ourselves struggle to see equity as something either stable or imposed, contrived or enduring.

Understanding Plato's Justice

One of the central tasks of the middle books of the *Republic* is to develop Socrates's argument that justice is a steady, rational principle. Even those who have never read a word of Plato's dialogues may well be familiar with a key idea laid out in this part of the *Republic*—namely, the idea of Platonic forms. Notoriously difficult to describe directly, Plato has Socrates walk through a few metaphorical illustrations of these abstract forms, which include concepts like the form of the good and the form of the beautiful.

Perhaps the most famous and evocative episode in this middle section is the so-called Allegory of the Cave, and it can kick-start our dive into Plato's theory of justice. In that vignette,

Plato tells a story about a group of humans who live underground, knowing only the deceptive shadows projected onto a wall in front of them. "They have been there since childhood," he writes, "with their necks and legs fettered, so that they are fixed in the same place, able to see only in front of them."[8] Among them is the philosopher-to-be, who is "dragged . . . away from there by force, up the rough, steep path" out of the cave. He would be "pained and irritated" at having to abandon the murky shadows of his subterranean existence and going to see with clarity and brilliance the truths of the sunlit world.[9] But after being both literally and intellectually enlightened, this wise philosopher—a rarity, Socrates thinks, among his fellow citizens—would then have to be forced to return to the cave dwellers, where the unenlightened rabble will likely resist his novel, strange, and literally otherworldly ideas. Himself a scathing critic of democracy and political equality, Plato here hints at one justification for rule by "philosopher-kings," the monarchic experts whose unpopular philosophical insights make them alone fit to govern an uneducated society from their privileged perch.

Even if the Allegory of the Cave captures readers' imagination with its narrative drama, it appears in the *Republic* as a clarification or perhaps an elaboration of a rather drier explanation of Plato's forms that immediately precedes it. At the end of Book Six of the *Republic*, just a few pages before Socrates introduces the Allegory of the Cave, he sketches his idea of the forms with the metaphor of the "divided line." The line offers little in the way of character development or a narrative arc (so readers may be inclined to skip over it), but it is invaluable for understanding the forms that are central to Plato's thinking. In short, the divided line gives a visual breakdown of the categories of things that exist in the world and their "degree of truthfulness": for instance, optical illusions are "less truthful" than physical objects. The line sets out these rankings by means of increasingly specific divisions. First and foremost, the line divides all existence into "the visible" and "the intelligible," broad classes that include, for the former, physical objects and physical phenomena, and for the latter, ideas and concepts. Sometimes these two categories are instead called the "phenomenal" and the "noumenal"—derived from the Greek verbs *phainesthai* (or "to appear to the senses") and *noein* (or "to apprehend with the mind"). The "visible" realm includes things like leaves on trees, shadows on the ground, and colors in the sky, all "phenomena" of our physical experience of the world. The "intelligible" realm, by contrast, includes things like right angles, the concept of balance, and the good.

But Plato does not stop with this primary division. He then splits each of these larger sections—the visible and the intelligible—into two subsections "in terms . . . of relative clarity and opacity."[10] For the visible, the lower subsection is "images" (*eikones*, the root of our English word *icons*), which includes shadows and reflections. The higher subsection includes "the originals of these images, namely, the animals around us, all the plants, and the whole class of manufactured things."[11] Not merely a division about the appearance of things, Plato's split between "images" and their "originals" is also framed as a split in "reality" and truthfulness: a reflection of a tiger is somehow "less true" or "less real" than a flesh-and-blood tiger, as is a shadow of an oak tree compared with a tangible, sturdy trunk.

Socrates tees up this careful distinction between "images" and "originals" in the visible realm as a parallel to his separation of categories in the intelligible realm. This second separation is much harder to grasp—we can give a quick account first and then return to some of the more difficult points. He wants "to distinguish the intelligible part of that which is, the part studied by the science of dialectic, as clearer than the part studied by the so-called sciences."[12] These "so-called sciences," Socrates clarifies, include topics like "geometry, calculation and the like," all of which need to "hypothesize the odd and the even, the various figures, the three kinds of angles."[13] Mathematicians, moreover, advance these assumptions and "don't think it necessary to give any account of them, either to themselves or to others, as if they were clear to everyone."[14] In the other part of the intelligible realm, however, there are no hypotheses and no assumptions. The process of "dialectic"—a word related to "dialogue" and best understood as a kind of interrogation—"does not consider these hypotheses as first principles but truly as hypotheses," keeping them open to skeptical questioning.[15] "Sciences," in Plato's eyes, need to start from what we today might call "givens," whereas matters of dialectic take nothing as a safe assumption.

This distinction, technical as it may seem, is crucial for Plato. First, he wants to draw some similarities between our concept of mathematics and his theory of the forms. Perhaps this coupling lends some credence to the apocryphal inscription at the entrance to Plato's Academy: "Let no one untrained in geometry enter here."[16] But inasmuch as mathematics is a relative of the forms, Plato wants to persuade us of a difference, one that my students have often found controversial. Not quite ascending to the truthfulness and "reality" of the forms, mathematics—in Plato's view—relies on "hypotheses" that go unquestioned. It is true, in fact, that theoretical mathematicians often rely on assumed axioms, like Giuseppe Peano's "postulates" that undergird the basic operations of arithmetic: we need to assume the existence of the natural number 0, for instance. My students have also recoiled at the idea that mathematics is somehow "not exactly true" or even "constructed": Aren't odd numbers and arithmetic sums actually, objectively *real*?

These axiomatic views of mathematics provide a helpful point of contrast to Plato's forms. According to his metaphor of the divided line, there are intelligible, non-hypothetical concepts that do not rely on these human constructions, concepts that can withstand scrutiny because they simply exist and are true. At least in my pedagogical experience, this is where Plato confounds the intuitions of modern readers. The concepts that occupy the "more real" section of the intelligible realm are concepts like beauty, justice, and goodness, whereas the "less real" section contains concepts like geometry and arithmetic. That is, Plato wants us to see there is something more stable, independent, and "objective" about justice and goodness compared with our merely "hypothetical" ideas like mathematics. Forms, unlike mathematical theorems, do not demand that we agree to unproven "hypotheses" or axioms but instead build on tested truths. They are, in a word, independent of us.

One final, related point here is that Plato sees these distinctions as both metaphysical and epistemological—his divided line concerns both what justice "is" and how well we can "know" it. More precisely, Plato links the degree of truthful reality in each type of object with the stability of our knowledge of it. He contends that we use "understanding" (*noēsis*) when we grasp the forms of justice and beauty, but we merely use "imagination" (*eikasia*) when we grasp the "images" of shadows and reflections. Etymologically, Plato links *eikones*—his word for those illusions, or "icons"—to our psychological relationship with them. We don't "understand" shadows; we merely "imagine" them. And we don't "imagine" the forms, but we "understand" them. This *noēsis,* or "understanding," is the strongest, most truthful kind of knowledge we can achieve in Plato's model. Even our comprehension of mathematical concepts like geometry, which Plato calls *dianoia,* or "thought," falls short of *noēsis,* just as the reality of mathematics is somehow inferior to the reality of the form of the good.

Our sketch of the divided line may seem peripheral to the debate between Socrates and Thrasymachus, but Plato's thoroughly intellectualized view of concepts like goodness and justice brings us back to those central, perennial questions introduced in the *Republic*'s first book: What is justice? Where does it come from? How can we come to understand its rules and goals? Plato's insistence that justice is a stable, intelligible form—even more stable than mathematics—leads us to provocative answers. In this view, justice enjoys utmost permanence; it's not a convention or a Thrasymachean imposition. When Thrasymachus contends that justice is simply the advantage of the stronger, bent according to the preferences of rulers, he speaks not of real justice but of an ersatz imposter.

By presenting real justice as an "intelligible," transcendental concept rather than a political construction, Plato's divided line also renders ethical questions as epistemological ones: we can't simply "make up" justice, but we can try to understand it. We don't impose it; we study it. Indeed, when Plato considers how we come to be just, he underscores that becoming just is first and foremost a problem of theoretical, conceptual knowledge: "The form of the good is the most important thing to learn about, and . . . it's by their relation to it that just things and the others become useful and beneficial."[17] Only by learning about justice—in the sense of the "understanding," or *noēsis*, of the divided line—can people themselves become more just. And since those of us who do not understand the heights of the divided line "have no adequate knowledge of" goodness and justice, we are liable to act unjustly.[18] This intellectualized notion of justice can also help us comprehend one of the more baffling claims of Socrates—namely, that no one does wrong willingly. Even if we happen to act justly without this knowledge, Socrates is hesitant to give too much credit for accidental good behavior: "Haven't you noticed that beliefs without knowledge are all shameful and ugly things, since the best of them are blind? Do you think that those who have a true belief without understanding are any different from blind people who happen to travel the right road?"[19] For those of us who have yet to grasp the forms—that is, pretty much all of us—we are still wandering blindly and only occasionally knocking into justice in our ethical meanderings.

One thing that is clear, however, is that Socrates advances a notion of justice far removed from our own intuitions and cultural practices. Modern societies often see justice as something determined and enacted in the courtroom and in the police station, not in the philosopher's study. But just as the philosopher is dragged out of the cave, Socrates wants us to drag justice out of the mad scramble of politics. We should also keep in view Socrates's pointed contrast with Thrasymachus: Socrates's philosophical exposition of transcendent, immutable notions of justice is laid out as a rejection of Thrasymachus's monstrous outburst about instrumental, cynical politics. Indeed, for Thrasymachus, justice is simply whatever a competent ruler says it is, and those who are naive enough to abide by a system of justice deserve to be ruled by it. Let's hear from Thrasymachus once more: "You believe that rulers in cities—true rulers, that is—think about their subjects differently than one does about sheep, and that night and day they think of something besides their own advantage. You are so far from understanding about justice and what's just, about injustice and what's unjust, that you do not realize that justice is really the good of another, the advantage of the stronger and the ruler, and harmful to the one who obeys and serves. . . . A just man always gets less than an unjust one."[20]

Instead of viewing justice as a transcendental, immutable form, Thrasymachus positions it as something constructed—and constructed for someone's own selfish purpose. The central issue for Thrasymachus, then, is who gets to design that purpose and whose interests are advanced. If a ruler is a competent, "true ruler," he will impose his own self-serving notion of "justice" on his subjects. And those subjects, like sheep who thoughtlessly obey their shepherd up to the point of their slaughter, unwittingly advance his interests while abandoning their own. Thrasymachean "justice," then, is hardly some virtuous ideal; instead, it is "really the good of another," a malleable cruelty anchored in the "visible," bloody basement of the divided line.

Imprecision and the Aristotelian Rebuttal

Even in the ancient world, Plato's theories were not universally accepted. In the middle of the *Republic*, Socrates admits that "much of what we are saying, since it is contrary to custom, would incite ridicule if it were carried out in practice as we've described."[21] As Thrasymachus's hostility toward Socrates makes clear, too, the class of philosophers among "the Greeks" was not a monolithic group. There were rigorous debates about the nature of justice, to say nothing of other vanguard theories like the atomist physics of Democritus, the radical defense of pleasure by Epicurus, or the rejection of the traditional Greek gods by Xenophanes of Colophon. Although Plato's theory of transcendent, immutable forms has proven especially durable for over two millennia—serving as an important inspiration for early Christians like Augustine—it is by no means the only framework stemming from the ancient Greek world that wrangles with concepts like goodness and justice.[22]

A conflict surrounding the nature and practice of justice would serve as one of the central disagreements between Plato and his own star student, a young immigrant to Athens by the name of Aristotle. At one point considered an obvious successor for leading Plato's Academy, Aristotle founded a school of his own, the Lyceum, perhaps stemming from his anger at Plato's decision to install his own nephew Speusippus—rather than Aristotle—as his successor. But even if Aristotle abandoned the Platonic Academy, he nevertheless bears the marks of his Platonic training: he, like Plato, espouses a belief in a divided soul, advocates for state censorship of poetry, and views democracy with some measure of suspicion.[23]

Despite these significant commonalities, however, Aristotle's departure from the Academy was both physical and intellectual: he is not afraid to contradict his former teacher, and, crucially for our purposes here, Aristotle rejects Plato's doctrine of the forms. In the first book of his *Nicomachean Ethics*, one of his most influential works, Aristotle rejects Plato's form of the good, a rejection that, in turn, will prompt Aristotle to radically reimagine Plato's conceptual, "intelligible" approach to justice. And these novel approaches to ideas like justice, fairness, and equality will ultimately lead him (and us) to the seeds of what would come to be called "equity."

Let's first consider why Aristotle rejects these foundational Platonic ideas sketched in the previous section. In short, Aristotle is suspicious that a word like "good" (or "just" or "beautiful") might have some reliably constant meaning across its infinite applications. He takes umbrage with Plato's "same definition of the good [that] will need to show up" in all good things, "just as the definition of whiteness shows up in snow and white lead."[24] Aristotle doesn't think we can find any such idea of universal "goodness." He explains, "The definitions of honor, understanding, and pleasure are distinct and different according to the way in which they are goods. In that case the good is not something in common and relating to a single form."[25] Aristotle gives the example of "whiteness" that can, in his view, be meaningfully applied to various objects that share similar appearances. But unlike "whiteness," the ethical judgment of "goodness" doesn't have some universal, unchanging meaning. What is good for the goose is not, in fact, good for the gander.

It's worth emphasizing that Aristotle doesn't reject the idea of "goodness" root and branch. He just insists on a flexible notion of goodness, one that is good for different reasons to different people in different circumstances. There simply isn't one idea or form that would be useful or even coherent for all its applications. Aristotle stresses how "it is difficult to see how a weaver or a carpenter will be helped in relation to his craft by knowing this good 'itself'; or how someone who has seen the form itself will be a better doctor or a better general."[26] Thread can have good colors, a house can have good foundations, and a general can have good strategic insights. But all these examples are "good" in their particular ways and according to their particular standards, and an inquiry into "the form itself" will not furnish the philosopher with the ability to judge or perform "goodness" in these various domains. Uniformly calling different things "good" belies their wide diversity, for what is good is also concrete.

To draw out the contrast, we might say that Plato's larger project with the forms involves finding the similarities and grouping them under the same umbrella term: "beautiful," "just," or "good." Aristotle's method works in reverse. He wants to categorize and differentiate, even in the face of apparent similarities. In fact, over and above the separation above of what is good for the soldier and good for the surgeon, Aristotle even sees our sensitivity to individual difference as a mark of sophistication: "For the doctor appears not even to look into health [as the good itself]; what he looks into is human health, or perhaps rather the health of this individual, for he deals with his patients one by one."[27] For the doctor, the "good" is the health of the suffering patient in front of him rather than some conceptual, abstract notion of Health-with-a-capital-H. And the more the doctor can be attentive to the particular patient in front of him, the better he is at his entire healing craft.

This impulse to separate, categorize, and even individualize "the good" underlies much of Aristotle's thinking in the *Nicomachean Ethics*. In his eyes, this attentiveness to individual cases comes with the territory of ethical thinking, and to try to standardize ethics under a uniform rubric runs contrary to the subject of ethics itself. The importance of grappling with this nonuniformity of ethical thinking is a point Aristotle stresses time and time again, and it can be found first just a couple pages into the book. Presenting a forerunner to modern academic disciplines that rely on separate methodologies and standards, this early chapter of the *Nicomachean Ethics* explains why any discussion of human behavior—including topics like politics or ethics—should sound different from a book of geometry proofs or logic puzzles: "Precision (*akribeia*) must not be sought to the same degree in all accounts of things, any more than it is by craftsmen in the things they are producing. Fine things and just things, which are what political expertise inquires about, involve great variation and irregularity, so that they come to seem fine and just by convention alone, and not by nature."[28]

These two sentences, brief though they may be, would tectonically rattle the Socrates of the *Republic*.[29] Anticipating his rejection of a single "form of the good" sketched above, Aristotle here separates activities that allow for great degrees of "precision" (*akribeia*) from those that allow for less. More specifically, Aristotle imagines that "fine and just things," including matters of political and ethical inquiry, "involve great variation and irregularity." While Plato wants to see the just and the good as unchangeable, transcendent forms or concepts, Aristotle instead sees them as shifty, waffling, and "imprecise." Contrary to our discussions of square roots and right angles, we should not hope to find some kind of firm, conceptual knowledge once we begin talking about the "good" and the "fair."

This rejection of *akribeia*, or "precision," of ethics is of paramount importance to Aristotle. The word denotes a kind of "exactness," "strictness," or perhaps even "persnicketiness," and Aristotle wants us to temper our expectations for how "exact" or "strict" or "persnickety" we can be about such matters. The same word reappears shortly thereafter when Aristotle tells us how we should approach subjects like ethics and politics, those that "involve great variation and irregularity": "We must be content, then, when talking about things of this sort and starting from them, to reach conclusions too of the same sort. It is in this same way, then, that one must also receive each sort of account; for it is a mark of an educated person to look for precision (*akribeia*) in each kind of inquiry just to the extent that the nature of the subject allows it; it looks like the same kind of mistake to accept a merely persuasive account from a mathematician and to demand demonstrations from an expert in oratory."[30]

Just as with his first comments on precision, these remarks on how an "educated person" should talk about different subjects are fundamentally at odds with Plato's views on justice. Plato's divided line closely links mathematics to ethical matters as two species of "intelligible things," and he positions the form of the good as something even *more* conceptual, *more* transcendent, and *more* stable than the stable-but-not-quite-perfect concepts of mathematics. Aristotle, however, urges his readers to treat matters like mathematics and matters like politics with starkly different approaches. He contends that mathematics (and perhaps also what we might call the "hard sciences" today) carries an expectation of demonstrable consistency. We do not want two plus two to "usually" or "probably" equal four; nor do we want the angles of an equilateral triangle to be "more or less" sixty degrees. Arithmetic should be exact and unwavering, and geometry should be a matter of proof rather than persuasion.

Aristotle sees that matters of ethics and politics will need to accommodate some irregularity. Since the "nature of the subject" of ethics does not allow for "persnicketiness" in the way that mathematics does, we may need to accept "merely persuasive accounts" about ethical matters when we encounter edge cases or complicated narratives. One might uphold "thou shalt not steal" as a matter of inviolable principle, but the *akribeia* of that moral law falls short when we encounter a character like Victor Hugo's Jean Valjean, who steals bread to feed starving children. Suddenly, the hard-and-fast prohibition against theft invites some measure of debate, consideration, or "imprecision." And the willingness to entertain this debate, in Aristotle's view, is the "mark of an educated person." Our ethical judgments should not simply be an automatic adherence to persnickety, abstract principles. Instead, we need to learn how to grapple with the often unavoidable "irregularity" of messy, flesh-and-blood existence.

This irregularity or imprecision, especially surrounding "tough cases" like Jean Valjean, again shows how Aristotle inverts some key tenets of Platonic justice. The *Republic*, we should recall from the divided line, wants us to depart from the "visible" realm to reach a more conceptual understanding (or *noēsis*) of justice. To rely on the *eikasia*, or "imagination," of our physical experiences to understand justice is, in Plato's view, a recipe for intellectual disaster. For Aristotle, however, these "real-world" cases enrich our knowledge of ethics and politics. It's a point that he underscores time and time again throughout the *Nicomachean Ethics*. Human beings, in their unpredictability and diversity, might sometimes force us out of a mechanical or rigid method of ethical thinking. Sometimes we come across extraordinary and concept-challenging individuals. Always an admirer of aristocratic lifestyles, Aristotle had a favorite example in the *Nicomachean Ethics*—Milo of Kroton, the famed wrestler of the sixth century who won the top prize in the Olympic Games. Aristotle considers the ways in which Milo, like today's linebackers or weightlifters, forces us to reconsider our preconceptions about matters like moderation and gluttony:

> So for example if [in mathematics] ten count as many as two as few, six is what people take as intermediate, with reference to the object, since it exceeds and is exceeded by the same amount; and this is intermediate in terms of arithmetical proportion. But the intermediate *relative to us* should not be

taken in this way; for if ten *minae* [a unit of measurement] in weight is a large amount for a particular person to eat and two a small amount, the trainer will not prescribe six *minae*, because perhaps this is too large for the person who will be taking it, or small—small for Milo, large for the person just beginning his training.[31]

Aristotle here relies on his famous notion of the mean or intermediate to determine what is ethically appropriate: one should be courageous but not too courageous, somewhere between meek and rash. It's best to be somewhat frugal rather than stingy or wasteful. Oftentimes, these judgments are no mere mathematical averages but instead should be "relative to" a person. In the nutritional lens here, we should not simply take a standardized, mathematical approach to determining the "appropriate" number of calories in a healthy diet, especially when we encounter extraordinary athletes like Milo (or, for that matter, a weakling novice). Olympic competitors—or the track-and-field stars devouring carbohydrates during my own classes—have particular needs that a formulaic, strict *akribeia* would fail to accommodate.

Of course, there is much more to say about Aristotle's ethical theory, and his comments on precision amount to just one of many departures he makes from his Platonist training. Perhaps the best summary he himself provides for these many developments comes in Book Two of the *Nicomachean Ethics*, where he describes his goal of ethical training. He hopes to cultivate in his Peripatetic students "a disposition issuing in decisions, depending on intermediacy of the kind relative to us, this being determined by rational prescription and in the way in which the wise person would determine it."[32] This dense sentence leaves us much to excavate, including Aristotle's well-known attention to "dispositions," or habits, as well as his aforementioned interest in "intermediates." But for our present discussion, which will shortly lead us to the concept of equity, we should simply acknowledge how Aristotle again draws attention to the individual case ("relative to us") over the purely abstract rule and his understanding that these individual cases will ultimately rely on a person to "issue a decision" rooted in some kind of "rational prescription." In other words, Aristotle foregrounds here the role of a person who makes careful decisions about these ethical matters—not by following a mathematical formula but "in the way in which the wise person would determine it." Again and again, Aristotle underscores how good ethical decision-making needs to attend to particular circumstances and particular people, a thorough rejection of the conceptual frame of justice as a form at the philosophical summit of Plato's divided line.

Before we turn for a moment to Aristotle's foundational theory of equity, I want to point to some important and difficult wrinkles in his ethical framework, at least as I have briefly sketched it here. First and foremost, many later thinkers simply reject Aristotle's turn away from stable and universal ethical concepts. In the ancient world, the Stoics would come to see the rational ordering of the cosmos—seen in physical laws, for instance—as an analogue for objective, unchanging moral laws. In a more modern context, Immanuel Kant would devise the "categorical imperative" as a binding moral law on any rational agent and one that could never be violated in seductive "edge cases." In Kant's eyes, "thou shalt not steal" really means what it says, no matter what Victor Hugo has to say about it. One important contention, especially for thinkers like Kant, who want to draw a distinction between objective "morality" and subjective ideas of ethical judgment, is Aristotle's reliance on someone charged with making "decisions" as we would hope someone would. Who exactly are these judging individuals, and how are they selected? Courtroom judges as well as other empowered individuals are sometimes selected by corrupt processes, and their judgments are borne out of biases and questionable motives. By placing ethics in the hands of powerful decision-makers, is Aristotle simply enabling (and even justifying) something like Thrasymachean justice, which is imposed by authorities on those foolish enough to accept it?[33]

These objections circle around some version of ethical relativism: justice changes with each person, ethical right and wrong depend on individual judgments rather than on firm rules, and so on. To be sure, however, we would be wrong to see Aristotle as a champion of extreme forms of relativism. It's crucial to recall Aristotle's opening chapters of the *Nicomachean Ethics*, where he contrasts ethics and politics with subjects like geometry. Aristotle does not encourage his readers to abandon the study of ethics and politics on the grounds that they have no stable or knowable content. He simply cautions against the demand for *akribeia* or "precision" in matters where it is not available. Returning briefly to Milo the wrestler, Aristotle wants us to understand that a "moderate" diet depends on Milo's athletic demands, but there are nevertheless general bounds for him—almost like an Overton Window of ethics. A daily diet of fifty thousand calories is wrong, even for someone like Milo, and so is a diet of fifty. But within a generally acceptable range, we must settle for some degree of imprecision in our determinations of what is "moderate" and perhaps even "healthy." Aristotle encourages us to abandon persnicketiness, but he does not ask us to relinquish all our capacity for good judgment. But how much to bend those rules, how far to stray from the norm—those are the essential questions that get to the heart of Aristotle's novel concept of equity.

The Soft, Leaden Rule

In the fifth and fourth centuries, during which Plato and Aristotle lived, justice was not a strictly philosophical project. The ancient Greeks were famously litigious. Some of their most acclaimed drama—for instance, Aeschylus's *Oresteia*—takes cues from the world of litigation: in the third play of that trilogy, Orestes goes on trial before Athena for murdering his mother, Clytemnestra, who herself had killed her adulterous husband, Agamemnon. Courtroom scenes can also be found in Aristophanes's *Frogs* and perhaps most famously in Plato's *Apology*, which dramatizes the conviction and sentencing of Socrates for "corrupting the youth." Since the law was such a powerful cultural undercurrent in ancient Greece, it should not come as a surprise that Aristotle takes his investigation of justice from the realm of philosophical inquiry to the scrabble of civic life. In the fifth book of the *Nicomachean Ethics*, he turns from his heady considerations of ethical intermediates and epistemological *akribeia* to the hard realities of "legal justice," the form of justice that bears on the daily doings of those ancient Greek citizens around him.

Early in his discussion of the law, Aristotle recognizes that "both the law-abiding person and the equal-minded one are just," introducing an ambiguity to the idea of "justice."[34] This ambiguity between the person who is just in their personal character or principles versus the person who is just in their adherence to the law hints at the tension we saw first with Thrasymachus in Plato's *Republic*: is there a principle of justice independent of our political context, or is all justice merely an obedience to the structures and rules imposed by state? For Thrasymachus, justice is simply another name for the obedience of the gullible and the powerless, but for Aristotle, obedience to the law is not just for fools. He allows both the "law-abiding" person and the "equal-minded" person to assume the mantle of justice and to be, each in their own way, just.

To be clear, we should not take Aristotle's claim here as an endorsement of blind obedience to the law. Elsewhere in his writings (in the *Politics*, for instance), Aristotle recognizes the danger of unjust laws—a law that unfairly confiscates property, for example, "cannot be just."[35] We should not obey laws simply because they are laws but because, in Aristotle's eyes, governance by laws has certain advantages over governance by human rulers. Centrally, Aristotle worries that humans are beholden to their irrational impulses and to partiality, so "anyone who instructs law to rule would seem to be asking god and understanding alone to rule; whereas someone who asks a human being asks a wild beast as well."[36] Substituting the rule of law with the rule of a human—a tyrant or a corrupt coterie of plutocrats—is trusting that a "wild beast" will restrain itself. The rule of law, however, evades this danger since "appetite is like a wild beast, and passion perverts rulers even when they are the best men, and that is precisely why law is understanding without desire."[37] Unlike the bestial tyrant—perhaps a nod to the Thrasymachean outburst in the *Republic*'s opening—the law rules "without desire" and treats citizens without fear or favor.

Still, in Aristotle's mind, there are some potential snags in an uncritical embrace of the rule of law. It is true that kings can become tyrants and senates can become oligarchies, but at least these human rulers can avoid the mechanical (mis)application of statutory language to a messy, unpredictable world. In the *Politics*, he summarizes the similar arguments of those who "think it beneficial to be ruled by a king":

> Laws speak only of the universal, and do not prescribe with a view to actual circumstances. Consequently, it is foolish [so say these critics of the rule of law] to rule in accordance with written prescriptions in any craft, and doctors in Egypt are rightly allowed to change the treatment after the fourth day (although, if they do so earlier, it is at their own risk). It is evident, for the same reason, therefore, that the best constitution is not one that follows written laws.[38]

The sensible doctor, so this argument goes, would never "bind himself to a written prescription. Things change and a doctor must be prepared to change."[39] More to the point, Aristotle recognizes that a doctor might encounter patients whose care requires nonstandard treatments. Echoing his exception-sensitive consideration of Milo the wrestler in the *Nicomachean Ethics*, the *Politics* here similarly urges that when we encounter extraordinary individuals, we will need to adjust our rules "relative to the person." Just as a medical doctor may need to make what we would today label judgment calls, departing from their regular treatments and protocols, laws will similarly need to account for individuals who do not fit the "written prescriptions" laid down beforehand. Aristotle takes this critique seriously, and he concludes, "It ought to be said . . . that a human being will deliberate better about particulars" than written laws can, so "laws must be established, but they must not have authority insofar as they deviate from what is best."[40] Follow the rules but don't worship them.

It's worth pausing to recognize the paradoxes in Aristotle's thinking here. He supports the consistent rule of law but finds the law insufficient for dealing with extraordinary individuals. He wants to empower decision-makers like doctors, but he also worries about the passion-driven and lawless tyrant. He wants us to consider politics and ethics as matters incompatible with "persnickety" scientific theorems, but he also equates the predictable and generalizing rule of law with "asking god and understanding alone" to govern our states.

It's precisely at this unstable, paradoxical moment where equity enters the picture. Looking back to the end of his discussion of legal justice in Book Five of the *Nicomachean Ethics*, Aristotle considers similar conundrums and introduces their remedy in a principle he calls *epieikeia*.[41] Similar to his discussion of the prudential Egyptian physicians in the *Politics*, here in the *Ethics*, Aristotle notes that "whenever the law makes a universal pronouncement, but things turn out in a particular case contrary to the 'universal' rule," it is up to us to "rectify the deficiency by reference to what the lawgiver himself would have said if he had been there and, if he had known about the case, would have laid down in law." Aristotle here considers how legislators, by setting down laws, need to make a general rule that anticipates future application, but since we could never predict all the extraordinary people, actions, and circumstances that could arise, we may need to "rectify the deficiency" of statutes by applying laws in ways that "the lawgiver himself would have said if he had been there." The principle that allows for this "rectifying" of the written law in these moments of deficiency is what Aristotle calls *epieikeia*, sometimes translated as *reasonableness* but also often rendered in English as *equity*.[42]

Let's consider a quick example of this principle in action. We can imagine that the southern Italian city of Kroton—home of Milo the famous wrestler—is suffering a drought, so the city passes a law to ration the scant food supply among its residents. As the law reads, each citizen of the city is entitled to six *minae* of food. But during the several months of drought in Kroton, the Olympic Games are announced in Greece, and Milo emerges as an extraordinary competitor. The law clearly states that each citizen is to be granted only six *minae*, and for nearly all citizens, this allotment is sufficient. But for Milo to prepare for his wrestling matches, he would need more than the law allows. Should the citizens of Kroton "rectify" the law, written without the knowledge of Milo's wrestling prowess and the upcoming Olympic Games, and make a special exception for his individual needs? The statutory language is clear, but perhaps "the lawgiver himself would have said" something else (but perhaps not!) if he had known about Kroton's ascendant challenger.

To better understand the general principle at play here, we can turn to Aristotle's memorable image, which itself has a durable shelf life among later jurists. He urges us to keep in mind "the soft, leaden rule used by the builders in Lesbos: the rule adapts itself to the configuration of the stone, instead of staying the same shape."[43] He hopes that in a way similar to this so-called Lesbian rule, a "decree adapts itself to actual events."[44] Here Aristotle has in mind "the architecture of Lesbos, where volcanic rock resisted chiseling into straight lines" and where the construction of sturdy walls required measurements and adjustments to idiosyncratic chunks of rough andesite.[45] Like these irregular stones, the irregular cases of the courtroom require that the jurist make flexible decisions rather than rely on the static language of the law, and in this way, *epieikeia* "surpasses the law through its power to accommodate the individual case."[46] In Aristotle's view, rules were made to be bent.

I continue to stress the original Greek word *epieikeia* rather than *equity* in part to underscore how the Aristotelian concept is not identical to the English word as it used today, most centrally as a matter of its etymology. First and foremost, it's crucial to avoid translating *epieikeia* as *equality* (which shares a Latin etymological root with the English word *equity*, as we shall see in chapter 2) since the word *epieikeia* doesn't actually signify a notion like equivalence or uniformity. The Greek root for *equal* is *iso*, found still in English words like *isosceles* for a triangle with two equal sides and *isotonic* for solutions with equal concentrations of solutes. Ancient Greek even has a word—*isonomia*—to express "equality under the law" or "equal distribution of legal rights," found in a famous debate about the merits of monarchic, aristocratic, and democratic constitutions in Herodotus's *Histories*, which predates the *Nicomachean Ethics* by about a century.[47] But *epieikeia* is not a strictly equal distribution or equality under the law. In some sense, in fact, the Aristotelian notion of *epeikeia* is a *rejection* of equality insofar as it justifies an exception to identical applications of the law. That is, *epieikeia* as a principle captures a sense of fairness that is fair precisely for its irregularity, so it makes sense that it does not build on a stem like *iso* that would denote "equal" or "level" or "identical."

Instead, *epieikeia* combines the prefix *epi*, here meaning "upon" or even "in accordance with," and a derivative of *eikos*, meaning "likely," "fitting," or "suitable." These components clarify why our dictionaries might provide something like "reasonableness" as an acceptable translation. *Epieikeia* is what is in accordance with a suitable appearance—what "fits," in an ethical rather than strictly visual sense. To my mind, the best English word to capture these etymological components is *seemliness*. Both words incorporate some element of "appearance" or "seeming," and the *Oxford English Dictionary* reports that *seemliness*, going back to the sixteenth century, could even be used in explicit connection to laws: "they may vtterly abolish good lawes, and liue against all lawe and seemelinesse."[48]

Another reason to think of *epieikeia* not as "equity" but as "seemliness" is to underscore how this element of "appearances" situates Aristotle against the Platonic backdrop we learned about in the preceding pages. The root *eikos*, a difficult word to render into English, is a participle of the verb *eoika*, which means to "seem" or to "be like" or to "fit," the last of which makes a connection to concepts like "appropriateness," "probability," and "plausibility."[49] Etymologically, these words also relate to the noun *eikōn*, which serves as the foundation for our English word *icon* as well as the Greek word *eikasia*. These words, you may recall, we have seen already in Plato's divided line, where *eikasia* describes our "imagination" of the reflections and illusions at the bottom of the "visible" realm—the dregs of Platonic metaphysics. This etymological link is a helpful reminder of the break Aristotle is making with his teacher. For Plato, mere "images" or "appearances" were the shakiest foundations for knowledge, and "acquiring an understanding" (in the sense of *noēsis*) of justice or beauty required one to leave the depths of the cave for the enlightenment of conceptual, "intelligible" knowledge. Aristotle flips the script on Platonic justice, underscoring in the *Nicomachean Ethics* that *epieikeia* is in fact "just, and better than just in one sense."[50] To act on the basis of *epieikeia* is to act on the basis of what seems to be right, even when (or perhaps because) the hard-and-fast principle tells us to do what seems to be wrong.

Equity as Ethic

We will come to see in the following chapters that it is specifically this Aristotelian discussion of *epieikeia* as the prudential bending of the law that serves as the foundation for much of modern thought on equity. Before we turn to those later periods, however, we should note one other dimension of *epieikeia* in Aristotle's thinking; indeed, his account of *epieikeia* as the bending of the Lesbian rule is only one of several discussions in the Aristotelian corpus.[51] If we look at the end of his chapter on *epieikeia* in the *Nicomachean Ethics*, we find that *epieikeia* is not just a principle of "reasonableness" or "seemliness" but also an attribute of a person's character:

> It is also evident who the reasonable (*epieikēs*) person is: the sort who decides on and does things of this kind, and who is not a stickler for justice in the bad sense but rather tends to take a less strict view of things, even though he has the law to back him up—this is the reasonable (*epieikēs*) person, and the disposition to act in this way is reasonableness (*epieikeia*).[52]

As Aristotle emphasizes in the very first sentence of the *Nicomachean Ethics*, his study is not simply about "expert knowledge" but also about "action and undertaking [that] seems to seek some good."[53] We shouldn't be surprised, then, to find that he considers equity as a kind of disposition for certain kinds of action in addition to a principle of legal interpretation. What is that character trait, and what kinds of actions does the equitable person perform? In short, Aristotle wants us to avoid being a "stickler" for rules. As the British philosopher Myles

Burnyeat argues in a seminal article, "The noble and the just do not, in Aristotle's view, admit of near formulation in rules or traditional precepts"; instead, Aristotle gives us a set of terminology for understanding "our ability to internalize from a scattered range of particular cases a general evaluative attitude which is not reducible to rules or precepts."[54] We don't simply memorize rules, but we "internalize" a kind of attitude or outlook that inspires us to act equitably.[55]

The notion of equity as a quality of a person's character comes to the fore in Aristotle's *Rhetoric*, a foundational work in the enduring Greco-Roman fascination with the methods and strategies of persuasion and particularly those strategies that are most applicable to the aspiring courtroom lawyer. It is also one of the other touchstones for Aristotle's thinking on *epieikeia*, one that will perhaps have a minor influence compared with the passages above from the *Nicomachean Ethics* but one that nevertheless will guide later thinking on the principles of equity. In that second text, Aristotle revisits the problem of written laws that fail to account for all future cases:

> What is *epieikes* appears to be just, and what is *epieikes* is justice that goes beyond the written law.[56] These omissions are sometimes involuntary, sometimes voluntary, on the part of the legislators; involuntary when it may have escaped their notice, voluntary when, being unable to give precise definitions, they are obliged to make a universal statement which does not hold for all, but only for most, cases.[57]

In some ways, this discussion in the *Rhetoric* merely builds on the general idea of *epieikeia* we have already seen in the *Nicomachean Ethics*. Here, for instance, Aristotle explains how "a lifetime would not be long enough to enumerate the possibilities" to which a particular law might apply in the future, so "one must have recourse to general terms" that allow laws to apply outside the exact specifications of their language.[58] But as Aristotle continues, he increasingly shows how, as Alasdair MacIntyre observes, "what is said about *epieikeia* in purely legal contexts holds of practical life and reasoning in general".[59]

> It is *epieikes* to pardon human weaknesses. Also, to look not to the law but to the legislator; not to the letter of the law but to the intention of the legislator; not to the action itself, but to the purpose; not to the part, but to the whole; not to what a man is now, but to what he has been, always or most of the time. Also, to remember good rather than ill treatment, and benefits received rather than those conferred; to bear injury with patience; to be willing to appeal to the judgment of reason rather than to force; to prefer arbitration to the law court, for the arbitrator focuses on what is *epieikes*, but the juror focuses on the law; and indeed for this reason arbitrators have been found, in order that the *epieikes* might win out. Let this suffice as a determination of what is *epieikes*.[60]

This expansive, multifaceted treatment of equity illustrates how the specific focus on *epieikeia* in the *Nicomachean Ethics* as a matter of statutory interpretation is Aristotle's developing of "a narrower idea from a broader one" that encompasses all sorts of behavior, not just matters inside the courtroom.[61] Aristotle's substantial elaboration in the *Rhetoric* shows that *epieikeia* could be considered reasonableness but also something approaching mercy or even kindness: he stresses that we should "remember good rather than ill treatment" and that we should "bear injury with patience." We should pardon misdeeds, perhaps out of the same line of thinking in the *Nicomachean Ethics* where the *epieikēs* person is one "who is not a stickler for justice in the bad sense but rather tends to take a less strict view of things, even though he has the law to back him up." And this portrayal of *epieikeia* as something akin to clemency helps tie together a broader vision of Aristotelian ethics in general and the notion of Aristotelian *epieikeia* in particular. As the *Nicomachean Ethics* reminds us in its opening pages, Aristotle finds something desirable in an "imprecise," "non-persnickety" approach to ethics. Since ethical reasoning is less uniform than mathematics, we are obligated to treat it with some measure of flexibility—to respect the edge case, to expect the exception. Based on this second treatment from the *Rhetoric*, we might conclude that *epieikeia* is not just bending the rules in any direction we please. It is, instead, to bend in the direction of mercy, lenience, patience, and generosity. To do otherwise—to bend the rule toward cruelty—wouldn't be persnickety. It would be monstrous.

Taken together, Plato and Aristotle (along with Thrasymachus) draw out competing notions of justice that go hand-in-hand with competing notions of wisdom, methods of intellectual inquiry, and even metaphysical views of existence itself. Whether we view justice as an eternal principle, for instance, or as a matter of concrete statutory application builds on our foundational theories of reality and knowledge. As we have seen over the course of this first chapter, these disagreements germinate one of the foundational theories of equity, that of Aristotle's *epieikeia*. By situating justice in the law courts and among the menagerie of litigants found there, Aristotle urges his readers to form an ethical theory appropriate to that messy, forensic unpredictability. And the capacity of an equitable person to accommodate that persistent messiness is, at least for him, "the mark of an educated person." The history of equity, in other words, is one that stretches back to ethical philosophy's earliest architects, but it is also one that stretches back to Greece's bedrock institutions of law and politics.

The interplay between equity's philosophical contours and the historical context to which that principle applies will emerge as a theme over the coming chapters, perhaps most sharply in the one that follows. There we will see how disagreements surrounding justice, equality, and equity were central to the Roman Republic's political tribulations. For the senators and consuls of those turbulent decades before Rome's transformation into an imperial autocracy, justice was not only a matter of settling particular courtroom disputes. It was a matter of organizing (and warring over) the very bones of society: the meaning of citizenship, the limits of equality, and the enduring tension between democracy and aristocracy. Those tensions and disputes from the Roman Republic have never vanished from the Western philosophical tradition, and as we will come to see in the next chapter, Rome's own terminology of *aequitas* never vanished either.

Chapter Two

The Roman Refashioning of Equity

Most people today do not ground their understanding of equity in a careful reading of Aristotelian ethical theory. There's no shame in it. They join the company of centuries of our predecessors who lacked access to Aristotle's texts and knowledge of Attic Greek. As far as I can tell from conversations with students and friends, our current understanding of equity is in large part grounded in memes, those "units of cultural transmission" that serve as shorthand for real argument in an era defined by retweets.[1] More particularly, these conversations both inside and outside the classroom often reference a widely shared, two-panel comic by Angus Maguire that intends to distinguish equality and equity.[2] In the left panel, three people—each taller than the next—stand behind the fence of a baseball stadium, each standing on one wooden box. The tallest man towers above the fence, and the middle adolescent can barely see over it, with only his head clearing its wooden planks. The youngest child on the right, even with the help of his box, remains below the fence's top and hunches in dejection. Under that first scene reads "EQUALITY." The right panel modifies the same scene by taking the box from under the feet of the tallest adult, who now stands on none, and placing it under the young child, who now stands on two. All three now see over the fence, and the previous panel's dejection is replaced with the young boy's jubilation, his arms aloft as he cheers for his team.

The tallest adult, too, raises a celebratory hand for their collective achievement. Under this second panel reads "EQUITY."

This meme, like many political cartoons, demands that its viewers fill in its argumentative steps. The psychological state of the child makes it clear that equality is somehow second-rate; at least emotionally, equity is the better outcome. But for every assumption it makes, the cartoon also raises important, if elided, questions. Is the goal of equality or equity supposed to be happiness? How do we decide which variable—number of boxes or quality of view—is most worth equalizing? Do not both images, in fact, represent some kind of equality? Do these three characters decide together to distribute the boxes in some way, or does the adult make prudential decisions for the two younger ones? If a second young child appears, how might the three boxes be distributed to achieve either equality or equity? The frustrated authors of a recent article on educational equity (a topic we return to in chapter 5) are similarly perplexed by this comic, and they ask an even more fundamental question: "Why assume that everybody wants to (or should) be watching a baseball game at all?"[3]

We might see this meme as an intellectual failure since it aims to clarify our thinking about equality and equity but instead just muddles the two concepts. But recognizing this conceptual ambiguity is a crucial step in drawing out the complicated history of equity, especially in its linguistic ancestry. In our etymological consideration of equity in Aristotle's writings, we saw how *epieikeia* stands in contrast to notions of equality (the latter of which use a different Greek stem, *iso*), and in this Aristotelian frame, *epieikeia* justifies *unequal*, nonstandard treatment. As the comic here shows, however, the distinction between these two concepts in English is rather unclear, and our contemporary language eschews these distinct Greek roots (*iso* and *eik*) for an entirely separate set of terminology. In our own language, these words differ by just two letters, sneaking an extra syllable in the middle of *equality* but nevertheless preserving the familiar *equ* root. This meme, then, suggests both a lexicographical and conceptual closeness of equity and equality that is absent in our Greek sources.

As it turns out, it's not the Greek terminology that has catalyzed so much confusion but instead the Latin predecessors of our English terms. The ancient Romans are largely responsible for the English confounding of equality and equity, for just like those of us viewing this well-known comic today, the Latin speakers of the Eternal City also used words of similar appearance, derivation, and meaning. Our contemporary language of equity and equality stems from a rich assortment of Latin words, all of which incorporate the same root. Consider, for instance, the adjective *aequus* and its antonym *iniquus* (formed by attaching the negating prefix *in* to *aequus*). As we might expect from our English cognates like *equal* and *inequitable*, the Latin stem of these words denotes something even, level, or fair; our most authoritative Latin dictionaries bear out our linguistic hunch, reporting that the adjective *aequalis* (*equal*) and the noun *aequitas* (*equity*) both come from the adjective *aequus*, itself equivalent to our English word *equal*.[4] Similarly, the adjectives *aequabilis* (*equable*) and *aequus* are related to the verb *aequo*, which means "to make level." And this verb *aequo*, in turn, is related to the noun *aequor*, which can mean generally any even surface but more concretely (and more frequently) the level surface of the open sea. What *aequus* or *aequabilis* has, in this etymological sense, is the uniform appearance of still water. An ancient text on the origins of the Latin language confirms this analogue. The first-century Roman encyclopedist and polymath Varro writes in his *De Lingua Latina* that the sea is called *aequor* because it is *aequatum*—or level—"when it is not disturbed by the wind."[5]

In its recollection of the calm sea, Varro's analogy positions this set of Latin vocabulary in stark contrast to the idea of *epieikeia* presented in *Nicomachean Ethics*. The Greek version of equity—viewed as Aristotle's flexible leaden rule—is one defined by deliberate misshapenness, whereas the Latin version aims at an undisturbed evenness or a straight regularity. And as we see in our own contemporary memes, equality and equity both appear as a kind of leveling or evening—the former of wooden boxes, the latter of unobstructed views.[6] In what ways, then, does the Roman *aequitas* bear any resemblance to Aristotelian *epieikeia*? How do these two terms, different as they are in their ancient metaphors, both feed into modern notions of equity?

As we will find in this chapter, the Romans themselves found these connections vexing, and the meaning of words like *aequitas* and *aequus* persistently carried some measure of ambiguity, waffling between the meanings of "equality" and "fairness." For some ancients, these concepts meant a true equality among Roman citizens. For others, they meant preserving long-standing inequalities and rewarding merit, however it might be defined. In the wake of these persistent disagreements, the history of the Latin term *aequitas*—and in turn, our understanding of equity—has been beset with some measure of conceptual vagueness since antiquity. Our contemporary cartoons, then, hardly unique in their ethical imprecision, join their august Roman predecessors in a long, difficult, and sometimes frustrating tradition of trying to define an idea of fairness, which, for thousands of years, has never enjoyed real, lasting consensus.

The Captor Becomes the Captive

Despite its towering architectural and literary achievements during the fifth century, Greece did not remain the cultural epicenter of the Mediterranean for long. Sparta subdued Athens in the Peloponnesian War in the late 400s BCE, ushering in an era when the Hellenic world continued to suffer from its fractured alliances and unstable internal politics. The task ultimately fell to Philip II of Macedon in the middle of the fourth century and Philip's young but ambitious son, Alexander the Great, to consolidate the Greek achievement and spread it at the tip of a sword as he marched eastward, crossing as far as the Indian subcontinent. Alexander presented himself as a Greek hero, fashioning a likeness as a kind of new Achilles, even importing Greek artistic traditions into his empire's far-flung territories (exemplified today in a *Ghadhāran* sculpture of the Trojan horse from ancient India, now housed at the British Museum).[7] But his conquests abroad would somewhat paradoxically hasten the decline of his Hellenic homelands. The larger the Alexandrian world became, the smaller the ancestral Greek peninsula on the Mediterranean would seem.

As Grecian power waned during Alexander's eastward conquest, a military and cultural power to Greece's west also began its long ascent toward geopolitical domination. This ascendant power, of course, was Rome. Founded in 753 BCE as a small farming town on the banks of the Tiber River, Rome would come to swallow the entire Mediterranean world, even conquering the remnants of Alexander's eastern empire at the Battle of Actium in 31 BCE. Twice defeated—first by Philip II and later by the imperialist Romans—the Greek world nevertheless persisted in these later centuries, never quite vanishing under the force of its captors. The Roman poet Horace understood this paradox well. Writing after Rome's decisive military victory at Actium, Horace summarizes in his *Epistles* Greece's unlikely persistence: "The captive Greece captured her savage conqueror and brought her arts into uncivilized Rome."[8] Himself an eager admirer of Greek literature, including the intricate meters of poets like Sappho and Alcaeus, Horace recognized that for all its military might, Rome did not invent a culture of its own but instead adopted the artistic, religious, and intellectual histories of its eastern neighbors. Zeus became Jupiter, Homer became Vergil, and Thucydides became Sallust.

Did the Greek *epieikeia*, then, simply become the Latin *aequitas*? The story is not as simple as replacing one word with another. Among the several aspects of Greek culture that would find a new home in Rome was Greek philosophy, and Roman philosophical thinkers were eager to adopt Greek thought, even if they were at times frustrated by the inability of the Latin language to capture the subtlety of Greek linguistic quirks like "middle voice" verbs, halfway between active and passive. These twin trends—Rome's enduring fascination with Greek intellectual culture alongside a rise in Latin as the *lingua franca* of the Western Empire—introduce challenges and questions for us as we trace the evolution of *equity* in the Roman world. The Romans borrowed legal and ethical frameworks from their Hellenic predecessors, it is true, but they had to render those concepts in new terminology, bringing conceptual changes in tow. In that sense, the Latin of the Romans serves as a kind of intellectual filter for us: it is difficult to trace our *justice* straight to the Greeks' *dikaiosynē* without the bridge of Roman *iustitia*, just as our notion of liberty comes to us not directly from the Greeks' *eleutheria* but through the Romans' middleman of *libertas*. Our English word *equity* similarly comes from the *epiekieia* of the Greek-speaking tradition but only through the filter of *aequitas*. In other words, the Romans did not simply translate *epieikeia* as *aequitas*, preserving unchanged those Aristotelian arguments for statutory flexibility and the visual metaphor of soft lead. They instead mixed this earlier notion of equity with their own thinking on equality, an etymologically similar concept that proved contentious amid the openly aristocratic politics of the Roman Republic.

These linguistic filters, moreover, were not faceless, soulless machines designed for Greco-Roman cultural blending. Just as Horace was responsible for translating those Greek poetic forms into his native Latin tongue, so, too, would Greek considerations of politics and ethics migrate to Rome in large part through the pen of Marcus Tullius Cicero. The definitive statesman-*cum*-philosopher of the last century of the Roman Republic, Cicero enjoyed a successful career as a litigator and politician. He was a so-called *novus homo*, or "new man," the first from his family to achieve the rank of *consul*, the top executive office of the republic. Alongside these professional successes, Cicero also took it upon himself to bring the lofty philosophical ideas of the Greeks into his Latin tongue. Today we have several of Cicero's writings, including those on epistemology (like his *Academica*), ethics (like his *On Duties*, or *De Officiis*), and theology (like his *On the Nature of the Gods*, or *De Natura Deorum*). We even have his Latin translation of a long Greek poem—the *Phaenomena* of Aratus—about the constellations.

As part of this wide-ranging project of cultural and intellectual translation, Cicero also wrote *De Re Publica*, or *On the Republic*, which mimics the similarly titled text of Plato in several ways. Like Plato's *Republic*, it is a dialogue among prominent historical citizens, and it even echoes the original *Republic* by ending with a perplexing dream sequence concerning the afterlife of immortal souls.[9] And like Plato's text, Cicero's *De Re Publica* questions the definition, value, and aim of matters like justice, equality, and fairness. What does it mean for a society to embody justice in the age of Caesar rather than the age of Socrates? What does justice look like in a culture rife with military conflict and bloodshed? How should a society as stratified, aristocratic, and chaotic as ancient Rome view the calm, ethical sea of *aequitas*?

Answering these questions demands first that we recognize how Rome never embraced equality as its defining national trait. In its earliest days after its mythological founding in 753 BCE, Rome was ruled by a monarch—sometimes a beloved figure like Romulus or Numa but sometimes an unbridled tyrant like Tarquin the Proud. Even after the Romans deposed Tarquin to establish their Republic in 509 BCE, they set up not a society of political equals but instead one of formal social classes and unabashed privileges for an aristocratic minority. From its earliest days, the Roman Republic reserved certain political and social privileges for the patrician families of Rome's upper crust—Julius Caesar, for instance, was born into the elite *gens Julia*, which traced its familial history back to the mythological era of Rome's founding. Even as patrician families later agreed to give more political power to the underclass of plebeians after widespread revolts during the so-called Struggle of the Orders, the well-to-do patricians retained vast economic and legal superiority and scorned the idea of true political equality.

This entrenched stratification turned out to be a ticking bomb for the republic. The enduring discontent of the plebeians ballooned when they lost control of their land and livelihoods in the aftermath of Rome's expansionist wars, and when reformers Tiberius and Gaius Gracchus tried to reclaim land from wealthy Romans for redistribution among its struggling citizens, the young populist reformers lost their lives just as Rome lost its stability. The Republic's political chaos would only worsen thereafter. The patrician Sulla wielded the blunt tool of dictatorship and marched an army onto Rome to impose his political and social reforms through state-sanctioned theft and murder. Taking inspiration from Sulla's brush with one-man rule, Julius Caesar later installed himself as *dictator perpetuo*, and after his assassination on the Ides of March in 44, Rome would only further devolve into imperial autocracy. But even before Caesar's adoptive teenage son, Octavian, became Emperor Augustus in 27 BCE, Rome had long struggled to stabilize its hereditary aristocracy and never committed to a strong form of equality among all its citizens.

Against this backdrop of political chaos in the republic's final decades, Cicero wrote *De Re Publica*, a work whose consideration of stable constitutions is no mere ivory-tower meditation. In the face of seditious populists like Catiline and dictatorial strongmen like Sulla, Cicero considered what kinds of political order might allow a state like Rome to survive and even flourish. Eager to channel the insights of his Greek predecessors, Cicero takes several cues from Plato's similarly titled work, but just as Aristotle did, Cicero departed from Plato in important ways. For instance, Plato famously denounces democracy, calling it a seductive "cloak embroidered with every kind of ornament," as well as other forms of government like a "timocracy" of military elites or an oligarchy of wealthy aristocrats.[10] Instead, Plato endorses a state managed by philosopher-kings whose capacity for rational, contemplative philosophy justifies their rule over their fellow citizens.[11] Cicero follows Plato in his critique of extreme democracy, but he rejects monarchy as the ideal constitution. Still allergic to the memory of Tarquin the Proud, whose ouster ushered in the Roman Republic in the late sixth century BCE, and wary of Julius Caesar's dictatorial ascent in his own time, Cicero underscores the dangers of one-man rule. He doubts that "one such monarch could adequately accomplish everything."[12]

The suspicion of monarchy, however, in *De Re Publica* hardly leads Cicero to a full-throated defense of true equality or *aequabilitas*. In fact, Cicero's text underscores what it sees as the gross injustice of treating all citizens in the same way:

> Legal equality (*aequabilitas iuris*)—the object of free peoples—cannot be preserved: the people themselves, no matter how uncontrolled they may be, are especially prone to giving great rewards to many individuals, and they pay great attention to the selection of men and honors. What people call equality (*aequabilitas*) is in fact very unfair (*iniquissima*). When the same degree of honor is given to the best and the worst (and

such must exist in any population), then equity itself (*ipsa aequitas*) is highly inequitable (*iniquissima*).[13]

Part of the problem with equality, as the unnamed speaker in the dialogue argues here, is that "even radical democrats apportion positions of honor unequally" and therefore fail to enact their putative goal of true equality or *aequabilitas*.[14] Advocates of this kind of equality, in other words, claim to reject differences while still embracing them. A truly democratic understanding of *aequabilitas*, moreover, would amount to a failure to acknowledge a citizenry's natural diversity (and therefore natural inequalities)—the full spectrum from "best" to "worst" citizens "must exist in any population."[15] In short, Cicero's text hints at an argument in support of aristocracy: Those who are best equipped, most talented, and otherwise most "meritorious" deserve to be given powers and privileges above others. To equalize everyone is to neglect those merits.

The passage here is not especially remarkable for its defense of aristocracy, which echoes earlier arguments from Greek sources like Herodotus and Aristotle. Its reliance on words related to *aequitas*, however, reveals the breadth—and obscurity—of this collection of Latin terminology. Cicero's speaker oscillates between *aequabilitas* and *aequitas* in this endorsement of aristocracy, so it can be difficult to figure out exactly what the words signify on an initial read.[16] First, we want to notice that the discussion here isn't interested in statutory interpretation, so we should not take either *aequabilitas* or *aequitas* to mean "equity" in the sense of *epieikeia* in the *Nicomachean Ethics*. Instead, this text considers the possibility and desirability of various kinds of equality in state constitutions. Advocates of democracy see in *aequabilitas* a radical leveling of citizens, reminiscent of the calm sea in Varro's etymological illustration of *aequor*. For the aristocratic speaker, however, this true equality, or *aequabilitas*, is *iniquissima*, the superlative, negative form of the adjective *aequus*: "most inequitable." When he writes that democratic *aequabilitas* is *iniquissima*, Cicero does not nonsensically mean that equality is not equal; he means that equality (*aequabilitas*) is not fair. When democratic advocates press forward with their extreme *aequabilitas*, those advocates corrupt "equity itself" (*ipsa aequitas*) and turn it into its moral opposite: the height of inequity.[17]

In one sense, we might argue, this aristocratic critique of extreme equality echoes some aspects of Aristotle's notion of *epieikeia*, even if Cicero's discussion here does not directly turn on matters of legal interpretation. When we are committed to the identical treatment of all people—including extraordinary people like Milo the wrestler—then we end up with "inequitable" outcomes. In Aristotle's eyes, Milo deserves more food than the average citizen, and for Cicero's aristocratic speaker here, the meritorious citizen likewise deserves more political clout than the average Roman. For him, redefining "fairness" (*ipsa aequitas*) as extreme and inflexible equality subverts the very idea of fairness. But in another sense, Cicero's text here exploits the ambiguity between equality and equity that we saw in the baseball meme insofar as both the comic and *De Re Publica* serve as critiques of the "wrong" kind of equality. Just as the comic presses us to move away from the procedural equality of distributing one wooden crate to each person, so, too, does Cicero's text press us to abandon an identical distribution of political rights.

The similarities, however, end there. Maguire's drawing implies that an equality of outcomes—where each of the three characters gets a fair view of the baseball game—is ideal. The aristocratic view presented in *De Re Publica* rejects even this second type of outcome-based equality. Rather than aspire to this kind of leveling, the aristocratic version of *aequitas* here would demand that an appropriate "degree of honor [be] given to the best and the worst" citizens, rewarding the individual worth or merit of everyone. Perhaps the child should see the baseball game only if he received good grades in school, or perhaps the adult should see it if he attended the child's school play. Or perhaps the equitable outcome for the aristocrat is to allow anyone to watch the game who can pay fifty dollars for a ticket.

Other passages in *De Re Publica* continue to build an aristocratic, merit-based view of *aequitas* as a foil to extreme, democratic *aequabilitas*, presenting a view of equity that not just rejects doling out identical resources to all citizens but also spurns what we might call an equality of outcomes. In one consideration of the shortcomings of the three canonical constitutions of classical political theory—monarchy, aristocracy, and democracy—Cicero explains how equality in radically democratic states is itself unfair or inequitable (*iniqua*) to the aristocrat even when it happens to produce fair results:

> In monarchies, no one else has sufficient access to shared justice or to deliberative responsibility; and in the rule of an aristocracy the people can have hardly any share in liberty, since they lack any role in common deliberation and power; and when everything is done by the people itself, no matter how just and moderate it may be, that very equality is itself inequitable (*ipsa aequabilitas est iniqua*), since it recognizes no degrees of status.[18]

This passage helpfully lays out how some modern intuitions about equitable outcomes differ from Cicero's markedly aristocratic *aequitas*. Even if democratic rule empowers a "just and moderate" people that can manage its state well, these political successes nevertheless come about through the equal political empowerment of all citizens, itself "inequitable" (or *iniqua*) on the grounds that it abolishes "degrees of status." Echoing the earlier complaint that *aequabilitas* gives "great rewards to many individuals," the state that respects equality is simply untenable for the Romans' aristocratic attachment to social and legal stratification.[19] Whenever democratic *aequabilitas* is involved, the aristocrat sees inequitable perversions (or flattenings) of civic order. As the classicist Elaine Fantham explains, these passages present *aequabilitas* as "equality of active political power and [as] Greek *isonomia* and *isegoria*. This is the goal of democracy which [Cicero's text] rejects as neither just nor fair."[20] We might say that Cicero's democratic *aequabilitas* echoes the Greek stem *iso* used for matters of strict equality. The late antique writer Lactantius, an associate of Emperor Constantine and himself renowned for his facility with Latin prose style, gleans a similar understanding of *aequabilitas* in his reading of the Ciceronian corpus: "I do not say *aequabilitas* in the sense of judging well but instead in the sense of leveling oneself with others, just as Cicero uses *aequabilitas*."[21]

Political theorists have long grappled with the tensions between democratic and aristocratic constitutions, and this chapter has no intention of resolving the pitfalls of meritocracy or the dangers of mob rule. Neither does Cicero's text have all the answers. *De Re Publica* is nonetheless an invaluable source for us because it shows us how contentious and unsettled these very terms—*aequabilitas* and *aequitas*—remain and how they anticipate our contemporary disagreements. Like our baseball meme, Cicero reveals how the distinctions between equality and equity prove vague and even subjective.[22] For some, *aequabilitas,* or strict equality, is the only way to achieve *aequitas*. For others, institutionalized inequality is the true meaning of equity. All of these words—*aequitas, aequabilitas, equality, equity*—sit at the center of Roman political and ethical debates, which themselves arrive at no tidy conclusion in Cicero's writing. Like so much of the Mediterranean world under Roman rule, equity itself would remain a battlefield.

To help clarify the Romans' persistently fraught notions of *aequitas*, we might turn yet again to Aristotle, whose influence on Cicero was perhaps even stronger than his influence on us. But here, Aristotle's import emerges not in matters of statutory interpretation but instead in his view of equality itself. In his commentary on *De Re Publica*, James Zetzel notes how the philosophical antecedent of Cicero's *aequitas* is "roughly equivalent to proportional equality in Aristotelian language."[23] What is this "proportional equality," and how is it distinguished from the "extreme" equality of the constitutional democrat?

As he sketches in his *Nicomachean Ethics*, Aristotle's view of "proportional" equality is the principle of treating similar cases similarly. Like people deserve like treatment. That is, Aristotle wants to set out "the distinction between equality with regard to the persons involved and equality without regard to the person; between the notion that the same treatment applies to everyone and the notion that everyone should have his due according to his worth."[24] Veterans deserve particular benefits not because of their status as citizens but because of the membership in a particular group. Earners pay varying levels of income tax not in the name of strict equality but in the name of proportional equality—progressive tax brackets presume that certain groups of people "merit" different rates of taxation to achieve this second type. Back in Cicero's Latin vocabulary, we might see democratic *aequabilitas* as a kind of equality where "the same treatment applies to everyone," whereas aristocratic *aequitas* is a "proportional" system where "everyone should have his due according to his worth." Indeed, this justification of hierarchy and "worth" recalls Cicero desired, nondemocratic equality that "recognizes degrees of status" and avoids granting "the same degree of honor . . . to the best and the worst." Proportional equality, in sum, establishes categories of cases that all deserve similar treatment while recognizing that other categories merit a different standard.

True to the *aequ* stem, then, this "proportional equality" still revolves around the leveling of citizens but only those who are themselves of the same standing. But there are obvious problems with this proposal. What kind of standing? And a standing by whose measurement? As Aristotle underscores in the *Nicomachean Ethics*, any "equality of merit" or "proportional equality" always invites controversy since people are often "not talking about the same kind of merit":

> Everybody agrees that what is just in distributions must accord with some kind of merit. But everybody is not talking about the same kind of merit. For democrats, merit lies in being born a free person, for oligarchs in wealth or, in some of them, in noble descent, for aristocrats in excellence. The just, then, represents a kind of proportion.... What is just, then, is this—what is proportional; and what is unjust is what contravenes the proportional.[25]

Elsewhere in the same section, Aristotle warns that "proportional equality" always incites political disagreements: "For if persons are not equal to each other, they will not have equal shares—and it is here that the battles and the accusations start, when either equals get shares that are not equal or people that are not equal have and are assigned shares that are."[26] We might all agree that we should strive for justice and dole out fair proportions. But what kind of justice particularly? And what makes those proportions fair? Aristotle sees that democracies assign merit to all citizens of "free birth"—giving all citizens the right to vote, for instance—whereas aristocrats limit merit to those with "excellence." In its critique of *aequabilitas*, then, Cicero's text worries that the "proportional equality" of democracy is unjust and unfair insofar as it indiscriminately rewards all citizens merely for being citizens. Instead, the aristocratic argument of *De Re Publica* advocates for a different *aequabilitas* that gives unequal (but nevertheless "proportional") honors, rights, and privileges to those who deserve them according to their "excellence."[27] Only the latter kind of equality, he underscores in his critique of democracy, could be worthy of the name *aequitas*.

What this "excellence" actually is or how it should be measured are matters that Cicero leaves unclear.[28] As Aristotle hints, such questions may be unanswerable. To make matters worse for us, Cicero also tells us how this vague concept is "an essential characteristic of a balanced constitution."[29] Such a "balanced constitution" is a central feature of Cicero's theory of republicanism, which aims to avoid the drawbacks of the three canonical constitutions by integrating their best features into a "republic." And when *De Re Publica* describes this superior type of state, it does so by foregrounding some blurry, even opaque notion of *aequabilitas*:

> I approve of having something outstanding and monarchic in a commonwealth; of there being something assigned to the authority of aristocrats; of some things being set aside for the judgment and wishes of the people. This structure has, in the first place, a certain degree of equality (*aequabilitatem quandam magnam*), which free people can't do without for very long; it also has solidity, in that those primary forms are easily turned into the opposite flawed forms, so that a master arises in the place of a king, a faction in place of an aristocracy, a confused mob in place of the people; and these types themselves are often replaced by new ones. That does not occur in this combined and moderately blended form of commonwealth, unless there are great flaws in its leaders.[30]

This "combined and moderately blended" constitution was a chief innovation of republicanism, whereby Cicero hopes that one-man rule could avoid devolving into tyranny, aristocracy into oligarchic "faction," and democracy into a lawless, "confused mob." One of this state's primary features is its equality, or *aequabilitas*, but as the ancient philosopher Elizabeth Asmis acknowledges, "What is meant by 'a certain great *aequabilitas*' is not explained further."[31] Earlier in the text, *De Re Publica* positions *aequabilitas* as an equality of a state's citizens, but perhaps here Cicero anticipates later republican theorists like the second-century CE historian Polybius, who views "the excellence of the mixed constitution ... in its stability, which resides in the balance of three equally powerful parts."[32] Perhaps, then, we might understand the balance or equality of the constitution here not as a radically democratic *aequabilitas* among citizens—which Cicero rejects throughout his dialogue—but instead an *aequabilitas* among the "combined and moderately blended" elements of the constitution itself, an idea that would prove influential for the constitutional design of the United States many centuries later.[33] What we can say, in the end, is that there is one kind of *aequabilitas*—that of radical democracy—that Cicero sees as a corruption of equity, but beyond that, he gives us little in the way of a consistent definition or metric of the "right" kind of *aequabilitas*.

These passages leave us in murky confusion about how the Romans thought about *aequabilitas* and *aequitas*—about equality and equity. Evidently, we today are not alone in our intellectual and political struggle to pin these terms down. Yet even if *aequabilitas* in *De Re Publica* shows intractable slipperiness—sometimes standing for democratic equality before the law and sometimes for constitutional balance—its linguistic breadth pales in comparison with that of *aequitas*, as we have only begun to see in the previous paragraphs. Throughout Cicero's writings, the latter term extends to all kinds of political and ethical discussions. It is associated with "all the cardinal virtues, namely wisdom (*sapientia* and *prudentia*), fortitude (*fortitudo*), and self-restraint (*temperantia*)," including a dozen or so other character qualities like *diligentia, honestas*, and *pietas*.[34] The person who exhibits *aequitas*, perhaps like the *epieikēs* person of Aristotle's *Rhetoric*, is one who embodies a wide assortment of ethical traits, including sympathy and patience, not just a refined sensibility for interpreting statutory language or for defining constitutional equality.

Aequitas, then, stands as an impossibly broad term to define as a matter of politics. Even so, *aequitas* ultimately becomes tied to matters of legal fairness, even specifically to fair legal interpretation. Through some of these specific applications to the world of forensic dispute, *aequitas* would come to serve as a bridge between those earlier treatments of *epieikeia* and later, Latin-inflected discussions of equity. By touching on practically all controversies of politics and ethics, *aequitas* allowed those Hellenic debates concerning the letter and spirit of the law—those we encountered in the *Nicomachean Ethics*—to enter Roman parlance.

As we will uncover in the following section, Cicero will begin to repurpose the language of *aequitas* for his discussions of courtroom strategy and statutory interpretation. For just as Aristotle developed his specifically legal notion of *epieikeia* in the *Nicomachean Ethics* by crafting "a narrower idea from a broader one," so, too, would the Latin of Cicero's time sometimes position *aequitas* as shorthand for the sensible, fair interpretation of legal language, even while *aequitas* might elsewhere carry the more general idea of justice.[35] Indeed, a particularly legal notion of *aequitas* "was well known to Roman jurists even before the time of Cicero, in so far as it was employed to restrain the harshness of the strict civil law (*strictum ius*) by means of actions based on what was 'good and fair.'"[36] This *aequitas* of the realm of legal interpretation, itself a linguistic ancestor to later English notions of equity, serves as the crucial link between the *epieikeia* of Aristotle and our own considerations of a "good and fair" application of justice.

The Letter and the Spirit

Cicero was an omnivorous reader. Not only did he revise Platonic theories of statecraft in works like *De Re Publica*, but he also—almost ostentatiously—drops hints of his extensive reading habits. He recounts in his *Topica* how while browsing volumes in his own library, he once grabbed a copy of Aristotle's work of the same name and, inspired by Aristotle's text, decided to write his own version of this "system developed by Aristotle for inventing arguments."[37] And to the befuddlement of students who have struggled with Aristotle's technical, sometimes inscrutable Greek prose, Cicero elsewhere praises Aristotle for "pouring forth a golden stream of eloquence."[38] His knowledge of these philosophical traditions was wide and deep, and he eagerly reminds his readers of his rich education at every turn.

We would expect, then, Cicero's intimate knowledge of Aristotelian thought to extend to the principle of *epieikeia*. Indeed, the problem that Aristotle isolated in the *Nicomachean Ethics* regarding the deficiency of legal language is thoroughly treated in Cicero's writings. In his earliest text on strategies for developing courtroom arguments, *De Inventione*, Cicero writes that "it would be the height of impudence for one who wishes to gain approval for some act against the letter of the law (*contra scriptum*) not to gain his point with the help of *aequitas*."[39] Here Cicero alludes not just to *aequitas* as a principle for guiding statutory interpretation but also to a separate set of technical vocabulary surrounding the well-worn tension between the letter and the spirit of the law—specifically, *scriptum* (or "piece of writing," from the verb *scribo*) and *voluntas* (or "intention," cognate with English words like *voluntary* and *volition*).

It is through this dyad of legal terminology—rather than the single notion of *aequitas*—where Romans would regularly apply a principle approaching Aristotelian *epieikeia*. Cicero presents *aequitas* in a "sense so often found in Cicero's speeches" as the solution to defective *scriptum*, and as Kathy Eden underscores in her reading of the same citation, he "follows Aristotle not only in aligning equity with intentionality but also in recognizing the limitations of any written statement . . . to take account of each and every eventuality" that may arise in various cases.[40]

By setting up *aequitas* as the principle or facility that enables the lawyer to correct for such limitations, Cicero's early recommendations for navigating the tension between *scriptum* and *voluntas* echo an Aristotelian approach that he had surely encountered in his studies.

While Cicero at times relies on the language of *aequitas* in these discussions about the conflict between *scriptum* and *voluntas*, the latter pair of Latin terms to which he alludes above is the more common terminology.[41] The attention to *voluntas*, or "intent," in legal matters predates Roman courtroom culture, and "the importance of an emerging concept of intention [or *dianoia* in Greek] for the gradual development of Greek legal theory and practice cannot be overestimated."[42] This Greek tradition would continue to flourish in Roman legal procedure as well. Even if the seeds of this focus on intent can be found in Aristotle's writings, he often served as a secondary reference point for Roman lawyers in this particular regard. Foremost among their sources was instead Hermagoras of Temnos, a rhetorical teacher from the third century BCE. The most robust treatment of classical rhetoric among Roman writers, the twelve-volume *Institutio Oratoria* of Quintilian, makes Hermagoras's influence on the point clear. Quintilian tells us that even if Aristotle anticipated and influenced Hermagoras, the latter ultimately stands as the authority on matters like the conflict between the letter and spirit of the law.[43] Rather than foregrounding the Aristotelian terminology of *epieikeia* in his discussion of this conflict, Quintilian instead says that the Roman opposition between letter (*scriptum*) and spirit (*voluntas*) stems from Hermagoras's "*kata rhēton kai hypexairesin*, that is 'Letter and Exception.'"[44] And this division—between the law's "letter" and "spirit"—proves exceptionally durable not just among Romans but even throughout the history of English, appearing in both fourteenth-century Middle English sources and twenty-first-century legal commentary.[45]

When these Roman manuals bring *aequitas* into their discussions of the letter and spirit of the law, it usually appears alongside these coupled terms of *scriptum* and *voluntas* rather than as an explicitly Aristotelian idea of *epieikeia*. In his own study of the history of legal equity, Lorenzo Maniscalco straightforwardly claims that "*aequitas*, as such, does not feature prominently in the works of classical rhetoricians. It appears, however, occasionally within the issue of letter and intent."[46] He concludes on the same page, "When classical [Latin] authors used *aequitas* in that context, it seems to have had little to do with *epieikeia*. It was generally used to make the point that if there were justice (*aequitas*) in a case requiring a departure from the letter of the law, a judge would have been more inclined to do it."[47] On this reading, when Quintilian urges his students to consider "the intention of the lawgiver (*voluntas legum latoris*) [where] the most effective treatments are based on equity (*de aequo*)," we should see *voluntas* as a term of technical legal practice but not *de aequo*.[48] The latter is merely shorthand for the ethical sensibility of the judge who knows when a strict reading of the law's *scriptum* would result in inequity.

Indeed, classicists generally understand *aequitas* not as a technical term for statutory interpretation but instead as a broader notion of justice, echoing the breadth seen in *De Re Publica*. In his commentary on Cicero's *Topica*, the aforementioned work explicitly modeled on Aristotle's text of the same name, Tobias Reinhardt explains that *aequitas* "should be taken as a rough equivalent to *iustitia*," and it is precisely this "non-statutory," general understanding of *aequitas*-as-justice that might allow a judge to modify his application of the law.[49] Such a judge would see *aequitas* as a term alongside "*ius* (from which are derived *iustus* 'just,' *iustitia* 'justice,' and *iniuria* 'wrong, injury, crime') . . . [which] can refer to varieties of rules . . . that are not statutory, but are nonetheless binding."[50] That is, the principles of *iusitia* are precisely those rules on which the equitable person relies to adjudicate between the competing demands of *scriptum* and *voluntas*.

The problem, of course, is the vagueness of *aequitas* and *iustitia*, even in this narrower domain of legal interpretation. Like *aequabilitas*, which could perhaps denote a kind of radical equality among free democratic citizens or perhaps a balance among the constitutional elements of republican political philosophy, *aequitas* can likewise mean different kinds of justice to different jurists. For them, *aequitas* might be a license to depart from the *scriptum* of the law in order to enact its *voluntas*. But how? And what, specifically, is the justice that we try to advance? Just as democratic politicians and aristocratic politicians differ in their views of what a fair constitution should be, jurists of different persuasions will see the law through various lenses as they make interpretations in the name of *aequitas*.

It is no surprise, then, that contemporary viewers looking at Angus Maguire's now-canonical cartoon can hardly agree whether its second panel shows an accurate picture of equity. The Romans, it turns out, could not tell us either. *Aequitas* is not so difficult to define just because it has a complicated history as a word. More importantly, it has a complicated history as a *concept*, as complicated as the concept of justice that motivates Plato's *Republic*. Even so, some thinkers in the later Latin tradition would try to pin down *aequitas* to turn an unmanageably broad term into something more specific and meaningful. In the final section of this chapter—and before our move to the modern world in the next—we look briefly at how *aequitas* began to be associated with the specific notion of *epieikeia* and, in doing so, began to inform thinking on how and when laws could be bent. There are only hints of this reorientation in the classical period, where *aequitas*—as part of a broader notion of fairness—sometimes denotes the judge's accommodation of statutory language to difficult cases. The reemergence of *epieikeia* (rather than justice more broadly) as the root of *aequitas*, however, advances decisively during the medieval period and would in turn influence the early modern English terminology of *equity*. These terminological developments, of course, came alongside massive cultural shifts, including the fall of Rome's political dominance as well as the rise of Christianity, to say nothing of the complex transmission of Greco-Roman antiquity through Islamic intellectual traditions and the globalizing influence of European states. Treating all these histories is well beyond the scope of this book. Instead, we focus on one especially innovative and prolific writer of the medieval period: Thomas Aquinas.

The Medieval Bridge to Modernity

The Roman legal institutions of Cicero's day did not last even until the end of his century. The rise of Julius Caesar, his assassination in the Theater of Pompey on the Ides of March, and the ascent of Augustus radically changed the political and legal foundations of Rome. As one character observes in the historian Tacitus's *Dialogue on Oratory*, the political calm of an imperial *Pax Romana* wrought by autocracy also caused the courts to atrophy and oratory to dwindle from their volatile and even chaotic republican heights: "so long as there was no peace in the forum, no harmony in the senate, no restraint in the courts of law, . . . the growth of eloquence was doubtless sturdier, just as untilled soil produces certain vegetation in great luxuriance."[51]

It should not surprise us, then, to see that the language of *aequitas* as well as the problems of statutory interpretation also transformed during these tumultuous centuries.[52] By the thirteenth century, over a millennium after the court speeches of Cicero and the rhetorical lessons of Quintilian, "canonists . . . started identifying the idea of *misericordia*, closely linked with mitigation and Christian commiseration, with *aequitas*."[53] The concept of *misericordia,* or "mercy," predates Christian ethics, and it was also used in rhetorical and legal contexts during those earlier periods, but the association of equity with mercy reflected the larger influence of Christian moral teaching on Latin-speaking culture.[54] This general association between equity and mercy would persist later in the medieval period, but "the point is that equity in its broadest sense of justice, meekness, [and] laxity, was seen as the guiding principle of all judicial activity, including—of course—interpretation."[55] That is, *aequitas* was not taken as a synonym for the Aristotelian concept of *epieikeia*, nor did it have an exclusive tie to the tension between *scriptum* and *voluntas*. It held its broad association with justice and even adapted to the specific ideas of justice found in a Christianized Europe. Somewhat like the virtues of faith, hope, and charity, *aequitas* assumed a place in the general dispositions of a model religious life.[56]

This broader view of *aequitas* as a humane or merciful disposition reflects some of the classical writings on *epieikeia* and *aequitas* that we have already encountered in these first two chapters. We should recall how Aristotle in his *Rhetoric* sees the *epieikēs* person as one who is ready "to pardon human weaknesses" and "to bear injury with patience."[57] These sketches of seemliness, in other words, extend beyond the professional activities of the courtroom advocate and provide a picture of one with a broadly merciful character. We have also seen how Cicero takes *aequitas* as an umbrella term for "all the cardinal virtues, namely wisdom (*sapientia* and *prudentia*), fortitude (*fortitudo*), and self-restraint (*temperantia*)," among other traits.[58] The moral vocabulary may have shifted during the medieval period's cultural reorientation around the attitudes and arguments of Christianity—giving the pride of place to virtues like mercy rather than to, say, martial bravery—but the vocabulary of *iustitia* and *aequitas* nevertheless persisted in modified form into these later periods.

It was only in the thirteenth century when this capacious view of *aequitas* as "mercy" would begin to regain some of its older specificity, focusing the term on the legal principle of *epieikeia* sketched in Aristotle's *Nicomachean Ethics*. Inspired in part by the increasing availability of Aristotle's works, including Aristotelian commentaries from Arabic sources like Averroës, Aquinas was the "first theologian to famously link *epieikeia* with *aequitas*," and he makes clear his specifically Greek understanding of this Latin word when he nods to Aristotle's "*epieikeia*, which we call *aequitas*."[59] That is, Aquinas specifies his Aristotelian frame for some of his citations of *aequitas*, even if across his various writings he continues to "allude to *aequitas* insofar as it is identified with justice."[60] With these references to a specifically Peripatetic tradition, this towering intellectual of the medieval period set in motion the eventual return of Aristotelian *epieikeia* as the foundation of equity, a trend that would continue into modernity.

This shift from *aequitas* as a general term of justice or mercy to a principle of a specific kind of statutory interpretation becomes all the clearer in these medieval sources. For Aquinas and his followers, the concept of *epieikeia* was not just a remedy for all kinds of legal "ambiguity."[61] Instead, a "point often stressed by theologians in their discussions of *epieikeia*"[62] is how it deals "with cases where the wording is perfectly clear, but it is also perfectly clear that its application would be harmful to the common good and to the presumed intention of the legislator to serve it."[63] Dietary restrictions (avoiding meat on Fridays, for instance) that, if obeyed, would result in death by starvation are a common example: the letter of the law is entirely clear, but the application of the law with a strict attention to the text would, on the principle of *epieikeia*, violate the intention of the lawgiver. In this medieval example, there is no need for interpretation of the statute per se since the language of the law is not unclear. Even so, the application of the law as written would transgress more fundamental principles of natural or divine justice. By appealing to this specific notion of *epieikeia*, a medieval judge might bend the Lesbian rule of the law around the exceptional case of the stranded traveler with nothing to eat but beef jerky.

It bears repeating that the Roman tradition had a robust history of considering the tension between *scriptum* and *voluntas*, so it is all the more notable that Aquinas resuscitates the Aristotelian vocabulary of *epieikeia* when these Latin terms were readily available to him. Perhaps his decisive turn toward this Greek terminology helps explain his limited influence among his contemporaries, for "it does not seem that the medieval concept of *aequitas* was influenced" by this Thomistic reorientation toward the *Nicomachean Ethics*. Indeed, it was not before "the early modern period that Aquinas' ideas on equity would be developed to a great extent."[64] But Aquinas did set off a linguistic transformation that, in later centuries, would come to undeniable fruition. In the following chapter, the Aristotelian notion of equity—one specifically focused on the problems of statutory interpretation and the just treatment of exceptional cases—continues to gain traction in England and the Anglophone legal culture that immediately predates our own. It was there that "equity enjoyed a revival through the early modern period, when it came to be used by legal scholars to explain the jurisdiction of courts of equity," and it is to these "courts of equity" in the English-speaking tradition that we now turn.[65]

Chapter Three

Revolutions in Equity

God used to speak Latin. Thanks (at least in part) to the translations of St. Jerome, whose Vulgate became the standard Latin Bible for centuries, the Catholic Church embraced the language of the ancient Romans as their own. Latin today remains central to academic fields ranging from botany to philosophy to musicology, but even in the fourteenth century, Latin's esteemed place in religious and literary culture was already beginning to falter. It was in that century that a Florentine named Dante Alighieri would compose his *Divine Comedy*, one of the undisputed monuments of world literature, whose angels and demons speak not the Latin of Jerome but the Tuscan Italian of their author and his neighbors. Even when Dante himself descends to hell in his *Inferno*, he reads an oddly novel inscription above its infernal gates: *Lasciate ogni speranza, voi ch'entrate*— "Abandon every hope, ye that enter."[1] Even the devil's architects, it seems, had begun to supplant the Latin of Cicero and Jerome with the vernaculars of the Middle Ages.

This pivot away from the languages of the ancient world to the tongues of everyday life makes it a little less surprising that the ancient version of equity—particularly the distant idea of Aristotelian *epieikeia*—remained unpopular in the medieval period. Even if Thomas Aquinas began in the thirteenth century to tie the Latin word *aequitas* back to the *Nicomachean Ethics*, his contemporaries were hesitant to follow his antiquarian lead.

As Lorenzo Maniscalco concludes in his medieval history of equity, legal scholars of this period as well as church "canonists had not drawn explicit links between equity and *epieikeia*, and certainly not explored the concept of equity by referring to the works of Aristotle."[2] In the time of the *Inferno* and Boccaccio's *Decameron*, the Attic Greek of dense Peripatetic philosophy stood little chance of becoming a popular cultural touchstone.[3]

Later centuries, however, began to look at the Greek and Latin classics with renewed fascination, and the rediscovery of previously unavailable texts sparked an early modern revival of the study of antiquity. Poggio Bracciolini's recovery in 1417 of Lucretius's *De Rerum Natura*—a long hexameter poem from the Roman Republic about Epicurean philosophy—catalyzed revolutions in scientific and theological views, including theories of atomist physics and materialist cosmology.[4] In the fifteenth century, too, Marsilio Ficino produced the first Latin translations of the complete works of Plato, giving Europe unprecedented access to ancient Academic thought. Desiderius Erasmus, a Dutch priest and one of the foremost scholars of the period, produced in 1516 a corrected Greek version of the Bible, the so-called *Textus Receptus*, which would in part inspire the composition of the King James Bible in the following century. We should not be surprised, then, to find that "the link to Aristotelian *epieikeia*, perhaps the most distinctive feature of the modern concept of equity, was explicitly accepted and recognized by lawyers only from the sixteenth century," when the study of ancient authors itself experienced (and caused) a renaissance in European intellectual life.[5]

We turn in this chapter to that cultural and historical moment, first in England, where discussions of equity embrace their ties to ancient considerations of legal justice and statutory interpretation. These links are evident even at the level of dictionary definitions. In English legal writings of this era, we begin to find the word *epiky*—a word no longer used today—which echoes the spelling and sound of that ancient, Hellenic *epieikeia*. In one sixteenth-century example, the *Oxford English Dictionary* reports that *equytye* was understood to be a synonym of *epykay* or *epiky*, and in another text from the same century, the crucial project of "auoydyng disturbaunce in the communewealth" asks us to rely on "epiky and moderacion."[6] This archaic word helped these English jurists articulate their views of fairness in their own era, but the word itself is, on an etymological level, simply a mangled transliteration of ἐπιείκεια. In fact, another example from the sixteenth century overcorrects its spelling to underscore its roots in the Greek alphabet, substituting Aristotle's original *kappa* with a *chi*: "epicheia . . . is proprely the mynde of the lawe."

While sixteenth-century writers had fashioned this novel (if short-lived) English word from their ancient sources, other authors of this period were happy to use unmodified Greek terminology in their discussions of legal equity. Their writings make it all the more evident that Aristotelian principles had come to pervade English thought. In his comprehensive history of equity in early modern England, Mark Fortier cites Edward Hake's *Epieikeia: A Dialogue on Equity in Three Parts*, a 1603 work whose very title links the English notion of equity to the Greek term of the *Nicomachean Ethics*.[7] Even more striking is William Lambarde's 1591 work, *Archeion or, a Discourse upon the High Courts of Justice in England*, in which Lambarde resorts "to [A]ristotelian notions of law's necessary generality and equity's association with the pliable 'leaden rule of the Lesbian artificers.'"[8] Some English theorists were so eager to display their Aristotelian view of equity that they borrowed not just his Greek terminology but also his evocative metaphor for the flexible application of defective statutes.

But Anglophone writers of this period relied on notions of legal equity that were "anything but monolithic," and Aristotle was not England's only intellectual ancestor.[9] In the wake of

Cicero's discussions on distributive equality, medieval considerations of canon law, and the blending of equity with *misericordia* and other aspects of Christian ethical life, equity could never avoid being a complex, multidimensional concept. In light of this complexity, these early English writers would link *epieikeia* or *equity* or *epiky* to the "mynde of the lawe" while also drawing attention to its importance for "auoydyng disturbaunce in the communewealth." That is, they nod not only to the need for statutory flexibility in accordance with the lawgiver's intent, but they also resurrect those Ciceronian controversies about the need for equity in civic communities. In their minds, as in Cicero's, equity bears on peaceful constitutions as well as on judges and their verdicts.

While authors may have begun to consider the role of "epiky" in "auoydyng disturbaunce" in their states, that did little to keep political turmoil at bay in these centuries. The revolutions and tectonic shifts in global power partly motivate the chronological jump we make in this chapter from the Latin of Cicero and Aquinas to the English of Hobbes and Hamilton, skipping over countless authors of continental languages and traditions in the intervening centuries. Historians like Lorenzo Maniscalco and Mark Fortier already provide an illuminating and comprehensive view of equity's place in matters of law, poetry, and religion in the medieval and early modern periods. Rather than recapitulate their work on equity's various and profound roles in European and English life, I intend to show here how a legal and political notion of equity—one indebted both to Aristotle and the Latin tradition—took root in England's legal culture and, in turn, found its way into the very foundations of American political institutions. By tracing equity's journey from the libraries and courtrooms of England to the Constitutional Convention at Independence Hall, we shall come to see how equity first became—and has remained—a central preoccupation of American political culture.

All Is Equitable in Love and War—Hobbes's Double *Aequitas*

History does not repeat itself, but its anxious chroniclers sometimes do. As we learned in chapter 2, Cicero wrote *De Re Publica* amid the turmoil of the late Roman Republic—decades beset by assassinations, confiscations, and usurpations. Cicero himself would not live to see the beginning of the empire. Just a year after Julius Caesar's death in 44 BCE, Cicero had his head and hands cut off and his tongue impaled in retaliation against his famous oratorical powers. Over a millennium and a half later, a mirrored sequence of events took place in England. Charles I, the English monarch, was convicted of treason and executed, and in the rubble of his rule, Oliver Cromwell established the Protectorate, a short-lived and tumultuous experiment in English republicanism. After not even a decade, England again became a monarchy upon the installation of Charles II. While the Romans chaotically ended their republic and emerged under autocratic rule, the British Crown conversely ceded its political supremacy to a republican English constitution, if only briefly.

These mirrored calamities find literary echoes in the political philosophy of their respective observers. While Cicero wrote *De Re Publica* in anticipation of the wreckage of Roman republicanism, Thomas Hobbes wrote *Leviathan* just two years after the execution of Charles I and the rise of Cromwell's Protectorate. (After producing this first English edition in 1651, Hobbes also published a revised edition in Latin in 1668.) In the traumatized aftermath of this radical upheaval, Hobbes presented his treatise on how to "erect such a Common Power, as may be able to defend [citizens] from the invasion of Forraingers, and the injuries of one another, and thereby to secure them in such sort, as that by their owne industrie, and by the fruites of the Earth, they may nourish themselves and live contentedly."[10] His aim was to prevent future disasters like the one he had just experienced. Immeasurably influential as a bedrock text in Anglophone political philosophy, *Leviathan* sets out a stark vision of how a society can secure these paramount goals of "Peace and Common Defense."[11] They are second to none, for in Hobbes's eyes, the alternative to a stable, peaceful society is one in which people live continuously in "a time of Warre, where every man is Enemy to every man."[12] In this *bellum omnium contra omnes*—the "war of all against all"—there is only "fear, and danger of violent death; and the life of man solitary, poore, nasty, brutish, and short."[13]

To avoid this apocalyptic *bellum*—itself a kind of philosophical ancestor to *The Hunger Games*—Hobbes wants to entrust the goals of "common peace and safety" to a "Common Power" or "sovereign."[14] But Hobbes's "sovereign" is no ordinary, hereditary monarch nor some unwelcome tyrant. As one of the foundational thinkers on the concept of the social contract, or "Covenant of every man with every man," Hobbes envisions that the sovereign is "one person, of whose Acts a great Multitude, by mutuall Covenants one with another, have made themselves every one the Author."[15] In short, Hobbes lays out a theory of a state grounded in the consent of the governed, those who have given up some of their rights and autonomy in exchange for avoiding the "danger of violent death" that plagues the state of war.

Hobbes's reimagining of the state around the consensus of its citizens might sound like a kind of defense of self-governing democracy resembling fifth-century Athens, but Hobbes understands that, against his classical forebears, he is proposing a radical and innovative redefinition of political life and even moral philosophy. His understanding of justice is an instructive example. Departing from Plato's view of justice (and other matters of political philosophy) as a transcendental, immutable form, Hobbes instead sees it as a matter of constructed, even arbitrary convention. At one point, he defines "the Fountain and Originall of Justice" simply as the rule that "men perform their Covenants made."[16] (Conversely, he defines "Injustice" in the same section as "the not Performance of Covenant.") Justice, in other words, is abiding by the agreements we have made with one another, nothing more. Hobbes is aware that his view departs sharply from his Greco-Roman predecessors, even while he accuses them of following the arbitrary conventions of their own time rather than discovering the Principles of Nature:

> In these westerne parts of the world we are made to receive our opinions about the Institution, and Rights of Common-wealths, from Aristotle, Cicero and other men, Greeks and Romanes, that living under Popular States, derived those Rights, not from the Principles of Nature, but transcribed them into their books, out of the Practise of their own Common-wealths.[17]

Somewhat paradoxically, Hobbes hopes to inject his political philosophy with a kind of clear-eyed truthfulness about how topics like justice, sovereignty, and political rights have always stemmed from covenants. That is, he wants to show that his "social contract" vision of society—one that is always consensual and contingent—is no mere thought experiment. For him, a true study of politics must be rooted in a study of the agreements we all have made with one another. In fact, politics has always followed this consensus-rooted model, even when more idealistic philosophers have claimed otherwise.[18]

This sketch of Hobbesian thought, although rough and admittedly incomplete, is nevertheless a helpful backdrop for showcasing the durability of ancient theories of equity from the classical world, which feature prominently in his writings. In his remarks on the "third law of nature" above—namely, that "men performe their Covenants made"—Hobbes goes on to describe his view of "Distributive Justice," which relies on "the Justice of an Arbitrator; that is to say, the act of defining what is Just."[19] This arbitrator, Hobbes continues, "is said to distribute to every man his own: and this is indeed Just Distribution, and may be called (though improperly) Distributive Justice; but more properly Equity."[20] (In the Latin edition of *Leviathan*, Hobbes uses *aequitas* as his translation of "Equity" here.) Demonstrating his aforementioned familiarity with Cicero, Hobbes here renders equity as the principle of recognizing merit, recalling the concept of distributive justice and all its contentions about who deserves what and for what reasons.[21] When Hobbes says that "Equity" is the proper principle for "distribut[ing] to every man his own," he echoes these classical Latin roots. Try as he might, Hobbes can hardly escape the language and labels of his allegedly erroneous predecessors.

This account of equity as distributive justice, however, is not the only appearance of the term in *Leviathan*. In chapter 26, titled "Of Civill Lawes," Hobbes explains how "All Laws, written, and unwritten, have need of Interpretation."[22] For him, the surface meaning of the law is neither obvious nor sufficient, and broad prohibitions like "thou shalt not steal" (as well as the minutiae of English tax law) always demand that a jurist apply abstract words to the flesh-and-blood world. This call for "interpretation," moreover, adopts some Aristotelian overtones when Hobbes elaborates how "it is not the Letter, but the Intendment, or Meaning; that is to say, the authentique Interpretation of the Law (which is the sense of the Legislator,) in which the nature of the Law consisteth."[23] "The Intention of the Legislator," Hobbes continues, "is alwayes supposed to be Equity."[24] This second account of equity strays from the question of proper distribution and instead trains its focus on the perennial conflict between the letter and the spirit of the law. Calling the "sense of the Legislator" the "authentique Interpretation of the Law" and setting an adherence to this "Intention" as "Equity," Hobbes returns to the questions of correct statutory interpretation first explored in the *Nicomachean Ethics*.[25] Never quite adopting the explicit terminology of *epieikeia* or *epiky*, nor relying on Aristotle's metaphor of the flexible, leaden rule, Hobbes nevertheless sets out these persistent problems of legal interpretation in a familiar Aristotelian frame.

These two passages from *Leviathan* make clear the competing, even inconsistent, meanings of equity that existed during this crucial and influential period of English political history. On the one hand, Hobbes "follows traditional legal theory in maintaining that equity regulates the application of general laws to particular cases."[26] On the other hand, he sees equity as a synonym for distributive justice; that is, Hobbes also shows how equity might incorporate "the specific moral duty of arbitrators to judge impartially" in distributing rights and punishments among members of society.[27] Even if Hobbes positions his foundational writings on English political thought as a break from the classical traditions that precede him, we nevertheless find that he carries forward from antiquity a notion (or, rather, several notions) of equity, a word that bridges modern legal culture to its various Greco-Roman ancestors.

That's not to say that Hobbes makes no original contributions to our thinking about equity. Launching from his underlying theory of the social contract, where a government derives its legitimacy from that "Covenant of every man with every man," he jarringly claims that "what counts as 'equitable' is determined by the sovereign's will, 'and not according to anyone else's reason,'" inviting difficult questions about the possibility of "true" or "objective" notions of justice and ethics.[28] That is, Hobbes brings to the fore the problem of *who* is empowered to make judgments about fairness and justice. Is it an erudite philosopher or the common people? Is it unearthed in the edict of a sacred priest or by the vote of a raucous senate hall? Hobbes gives radically innovative answers to these questions. In his eyes, the very definitions of justice and equity always stem from the sovereign, and as long as the sovereign can guarantee public safety and keep the "war of all against all" at bay, he maintains the right to determine these matters of political justice for the people who have agreed to obey his authority.

Hobbes's radical approach to defining justice and virtue through the social contract—rather than through Platonic forms or even an Aristotelian imprecision—anticipates some of the explosive issues of the American Revolution and the drafting of the US Constitution. In a nation designed around "We the People," should a concept like equity or justice be rooted in the consent of the people? Should an unelected judge have the power to bend the law in the name of "fairness" without first consulting an assembly of their fellow citizens? Is a citizen obligated to abide by the definition of fairness used by their government if they individually object to it? The end of the eighteenth century brought these questions to a tipping point when the Americans retracted their consent from the British sovereign, offering them the opportunity to decide who would have the power to define, determine, and execute justice in new political covenants of their own.

Courts of Chancery and the American Revolt against Equity

Sometimes reading *Leviathan* can feel like an exercise in speculative fiction: None of us has ever witnessed a primeval "state of nature" in which we found ourselves in a *bellum omnium contra omnes*. And when did any of us sign a contract giving some "sovereign" ultimate authority over our politics? Not everything in Hobbes's text, however, is a matter of imagination. In his lifetime, in fact, equity was already an institutionalized part of English life, and under its esteemed mantle, England had constructed courtrooms and appointed judges. Well before Hobbes's own era, in fact, England had established two separate, although complementary, judicial systems: the courts of law and the courts of equity. The courts of law dealt with what is known as common law, the legal tradition that centers the principle of *stare decisis*—literally, "standing by things that have been decided." Common law systems rely on judicial precedent, and absent a reversal of earlier rulings by higher courts, they strive for fairness and consistency.

Inasmuch as England's courts of law, rooted as they were in precedent, maintained a kind of judicial steadiness, they could also be seen as harsh and even mechanical. By deferring to previous prison sentences, previous fines, and previous executions, the common law courts gained a reputation for cruel consistency. As a counterbalance to this legal rigidity, England also instituted a court of equity; since this second court was the domain of the lord chancellor, the Crown's highest-ranking minister and head of the judiciary, it was often simply called the Court of Chancery. The Court of Chancery predated Hobbes and the early modern period by several centuries, and its function was tied to the character of the lord chancellor himself, who "was usually [a] cleric, familiar with ecclesiastical law and notions of natural justice, and instinctively concerned about matters of conscience."[29] That is, the Court of Chancery eschewed the systematic rigor of precedent and instead consulted the chancellor's "conscience" in its rulings, a principle that "is a hallmark of equity" in modern accounts of its development.[30] Echoing Aristotle's notion of the *epieikēs* man who takes mercy on others as well as the Christian coupling of *aequitas* and *misericordia*, the Court of Chancery employed a notion of equity that was "said to be conscience-based, moral, and discretionary in ways that the common law [was] not."[31]

Perhaps the most well-known case in the history of the courts of equity—and a historically important one for setting the Court of Chancery above the common law courts—is the so-called Earl of Oxford's case of 1615, which to this day is seen as "the foundation stone of Equity in modern English law."[32] The particulars of the case are a veritable crash course in English history, touching on Anne Boleyn, Cambridge University, and Queen Elizabeth. Setting aside some of its more obscure details, the case centers on London real estate owned by Magdalene College, Cambridge, which, according to the Ecclesiastical Leases Act 1571, could only be sold under restrictive terms. After an original sale to Queen Elizabeth, the land eventually became the possession of the Earl of Oxford, against the protestation of Magdalene College. This legal challenge brought to the fore the conflict between the regulations of common law, which would have prevented the sale of this real estate and therefore would have brought the holdings back under Magdalene College's ownership. But the original sale involved the queen herself, and according to "royal prerogative," she would enjoy a certain privilege or exceptional treatment, standing above ordinary statutory restrictions and ordinary precedents.

This tension between common law and extraordinary equity found a parallel in a conflict between two prominent legal minds of the era: Chief Justice Edward Coke and Lord Chancellor Ellesmere. Relying on the principles of common law, Coke saw in the Ecclesiastical Leases Act 1571 a clear prohibition on the transfer of Magdalene College's land. Ellesmere would view things differently. As the head of the Court of Chancery, Ellesmere "was committed to upholding Royal prerogatives, not least because the Court of Chancery had itself developed from the ancient Royal prerogative of mercy," and he overruled Coke's punctilious adherence to the relevant statutes.[33] Ellesmere found that the particular circumstances of this case, while nominally governed by the Ecclesiastical Leases Act, were so exceptional as to demand a different standard of judgment, and rooting his decision in the Hebrew Bible and turning away from what he termed "hard Conscience," Ellesmere concluded that "law and equity are distinct, both in their courts, their judges, and the rules of justice; and yet they both aim at one and the same end, which is to do right." Strictly following the letter of the law, in his eyes, would amount to doing wrong. The ruling of the Earl of Oxford's case, therefore, set equity as a standard of justice above that of common law, laying the groundwork for a separate—indeed, higher—court system that would ground its rulings in the lofty principles of natural justice and a "softer" conscience.[34]

This formal division between the common law courts and the Court of Chancery lasted until 1875, when the Supreme Court of Judicature Act combined the rubrics of common law and equity under the High Court of Justice and the Court of Appeal. But before England brought a formal end to its courts of equity, it had already exported this judicial model to its American colonies.[35] Even after the British lost control of their colonial outposts there, America itself would set up and preserve—in the wake of its revolutionary battle for independence—a system of government that in many ways resembled the government of their former rulers. New York, for instance, founded its own Court of Chancery in 1701, which existed until 1847, when its equity jurisdiction was transferred to the Supreme Court of the State of New York. Michigan also had a Court of Chancery, although short-lived: it lasted only from 1836 to 1847. A few states today maintain separate courts of equity, including the Delaware Court of Chancery, which oversees high-stakes cases in corporate litigation (including, for example, Elon Musk's contractual obligation to purchase Twitter in 2022). Even if the colonists succeeded in severing political ties to the English Crown, they were (and we are) still beholden to the linguistic and conceptual ties to England, and the principle of legal equity would prove no exception to this ancestral influence.

Although the Americans instituted Courts of Chancery in various jurisdictions early on, the authority—and even existence—of these courts was not without controversy. As Gordon Wood catalogs in *The Creation of the American Republic, 1776–1787*, the resistance to establishing a court of equity in America was sometimes fierce. Allergic to the idea of empowering someone like a lord chancellor, whose authority was tied to royal prerogative, the Americans of the postrevolutionary period were reluctant to invest an elite judiciary with the right to bend, twist, and overrule the laws that they had fought a war to determine for themselves. Wood observes how Americans at that time "were firmly committed to the modern notion of statute law based on legislative enactment"; that is, they wanted only the legislature—the branch of government most directly connected with the popular will—to be the corrective mechanism for deficient laws.[36] Especially after 1776, "only a social agreement among the people . . . seemed to make sense of [Americans'] rapidly developing idea of a constitution as a fundamental law," and echoing Hobbes's theory of a state rooted in a "Covenant of every man with every man," the Americans embraced popular sovereignty as their new country's inviolable principle.[37] To set judges as the final arbiters of the law and to empower them to overrule the people's legislative representatives in the name of equity was antithetical to the colonists' mission for self-government.

But even as postrevolutionary Americans embraced the role of the legislative rather than the judicial in enacting and correcting laws, they would inevitably come up against a central question in their deference to the legislature: "could this emphasis on reason and equity in their law be maintained without judicial discretion?"[38] Can laws, in other words, operate fairly without a judge to interpret and apply them? Especially in the immediate aftermath of the revolution, many sought to answer affirmatively. William Henry Drayton, a South Carolina signatory to the Articles of Confederation, would advise in 1778 that "in republics, the very nature of the constitution requires the judges to follow the letter of the law," even while he admitted that laws were sometimes imprecise or even silent on difficult cases.[39] Others continued to believe that "no axiom is more dangerous than that the spirit of the law ought to be considered, and not the letter," and they feared that "the same laws that condemn today, will acquit tomorrow, according to different opinions which different judges may form of its spirit."[40] The unavoidable ambiguity of legal interpretation, brought out in Aristotle's writings, was a nightmare for these newly liberated politicians. Revolutionary-era Americans, then, might have been "committed to equity as the basis of law," but by reserving judgments of fairness and moments of legal correction to "legislative enactment[,] they at the same time denied the judicial discretion that made equitable interpretations . . . possible."[41] For these early Americans, equity was a goal worth pursuing— the value of justice itself was not controversial. But setting its determination in the hands of judges would have amounted to institutionalized tyranny.

By putting their hope in the "legislative enactment" of their own representatives Americans took up the challenge first presented by Aristotle in the *Rhetoric*—namely, that "a lifetime would not be long enough to enumerate the possibilities" to which a particular law might apply in the future.[42] Rather than follow Aristotle's advice in the same passage that "one must have recourse to general terms" that allow laws to stretch beyond the bare meaning of their words, Americans instead pressed legislatures to erect sprawling statutes to cover all possible cases. Aristotle wants his readers to rely on the simplicity of a flexible, leaden rule and an *epieikēs* judge to apply it prudentially, but some Americans of the late eighteenth century instead urged the legislature to churn out a prodigious number of stiff, adamantine statutes to be applied only as they were written.

As we know from the *Nicomachean Ethics*, however, Aristotle predicts that explicitly legislating every edge case and every Milo will always prove unsuccessful, and as the United States moved further from the events of the revolution and toward the drafting of its Constitution, some Americans indeed grew weary of the project of equity-by-legislation. As Wood sees it, Americans of the 1780s started to realize that they "could not have specific legislative enactment and equity at the same time," and the multiplication of specific statutes intended to cover all imaginable situations ultimately "resulted in a confusion that wicked men turned to their private advantage."[43] As these laws became more complex, they became regrettable opportunities for corruption, and the goal of achieving justice and equity through legislation seemed increasingly untenable. At this moment of legislative frustration, Americans began to see the judiciary as a crucial instrument for securing a just and fair society. Wood points to a 1781 sermon of Moses Mather in Connecticut that echoes Aristotle's calls for statutory generality: "where civil justice is to be administered not by particular statutes, but by the application of general rules of equity, much will depend upon the wisdom and integrity of the judges."[44] Newspapers, too, began to publish essays that demanded judicial mechanisms "to soften the rigour of Written Law, and to act upon such parts of natural Law, as have not been rendered Sufficiently clear and plain in their Statutes."[45] James Duane, who served as mayor of New York in the 1780s and was appointed to the Federal District Court in New York by George Washington himself in 1789, gives perhaps the clearest account of this new attitude:

> When the main object of such a law is clearly expressed, and the intention manifest, the Judges are not at liberty, altho' it appears to them to be *unreasonable*, to reject it: for this were to set the *judicial* above the legislative, which would be subversive of all government. [But otherwise] the Judges are in decency to conclude, that the consequences were not foreseen by the Legislature; and therefore they are at liberty to expound the statute by *equity*.[46]

Over the course of the 1780s, then, prominent Americans began to embrace the idea of a judiciary that worked alongside the legislative branch but not one that supplanted it. When they realized that sometimes a law's "consequences were not foreseen by the Legislature" and that laws themselves were often not "Sufficiently clear and plain in their Statutes," the need for prudential but flexible application of the laws became evident. Strictly in those situations, although not "when the main object of such a law is clearly expressed," judges would need to employ their sense of Aristotelian equity in fitting the general law to the specific case. The legislature would still be empowered to draft its own laws, but in the event of its error, ambiguity, or lack of foresight, judges could bend their leaden laws around misshapen events.

Constitutional Equity in the Battle for Ratification

The question of how to pursue justice in the 1780s was not merely an academic project; it was also an intensely political and public one. Even as preachers and jurists acknowledged their state's need for judicial discretion, the new nation's citizens and constituent states would themselves need to be convinced of the same in the years to come. More than an intellectual debate shared among America's leading thinkers, the campaign for institutionalizing equity was part of the effort to ratify the new constitution, following its drafting in 1787 and leading up to its formal adoption in 1789. The most well-known writings in this campaign supporting the new Constitution were published in New York newspapers under the pseudonym Publius and authored by John Jay, Alexander Hamilton, and James Madison. It was in these essays—as well as in those of their detractors—that the early American debates surrounding equity most publicly transformed from one only about Aristotelian legal theory to one also about the mechanisms of constitutional fairness.

For twenty-first-century Americans, the story of these *Federalist Papers* is a story told in reverse: today we live under a document ratified at the end of the eighteenth century, so the controversies over its terms and structure can only be viewed from the position of knowing their resolutions. We all know that Madison was successful in convincing his peers about the virtues of the balance of powers in *Federalist* 51, and we know that Hamilton's argument in *Federalist* 84 against adding an "unnecessary" and "dangerous" Bill of Rights was read by unconvinced eyes. So when Hamilton asks in *Federalist* 80, "what need of the word 'equity,'" we know that his readers were ultimately persuaded that the word was, in fact, necessary for the pursuit of legal justice in their nation. Specifically, Hamilton and other Americans of the 1780s agreed—as Article III, Section 2 states—that "the judicial Power shall extend to all Cases, in Law and Equity, arising under this Constitution, the Laws of the United States, and Treaties made, or which shall be made, under their Authority." Building from the traditional division in the English courts between matters of law and matters of equity, Article III similarly empowers the judicial branch of the United States to consider cases in these two veins. As we saw in the definitive Earl of Oxford's case, matters of "law" would also be subject to the demands of equity. But without a lord chancellor, charged with executing the queen's judgment and dispensing her conscientious mercy, what might American equity look like? After rejecting so many of the political institutions of their English forebears, how would Americans come to enshrine principles of equity in their own society and governmental offices?[47]

Before we turn to equity's detractors, it will be helpful to first see Hamilton's defense in *Federalist* 80, the essay that deals most directly with the need for judges to rule through both equitable and legal jurisdiction:

It has also been asked, what need of the word 'equity'? What equitable causes can grow out of the constitution and laws of the United States? ... It is the peculiar province, for instance, of a court of equity to relieve against what are called hard bargains: These are contracts, in which, though there maybe have been no direct fraud of deceit, sufficient to invalidate them in a court of law; yet there may have been some undue and unconscionable advantage taken of the necessities or misfortunes of one of the parties, which a court of equity would not tolerate.[48]

The crucial word in Hamilton's prose here is *unconscionable*, a word that recalls the English Court of Chancery's mission to mitigate the harshness of common law on the grounds of "conscience." That very word appears in Ellesmere's ruling in the Earl of Oxford's case. Hamilton's chosen example of a "hard bargain" focuses on a similar situation. Here, he presents his readers with a contract in which "there maybe have been no direct fraud or deceit, sufficient to invalidate it in a court of law."[49] That is, Hamilton sees in a "hard bargain" a contract whose terms are clear and whose signatories were aware of those terms but one whose execution somehow would violate principles of justice and fairness. (A helpful literary example is Shakespeare's "pound of flesh" at the center of *The Merchant of Venice*, contractually owed by Antonio after defaulting on a loan from Shylock.) Rather than defer to the privileges of the queen, which grounded Lord Ellesmere's ruling in the name of equity, Hamilton simply writes that a "court of equity would not tolerate" such "unconscionable" contracts, even if they might withstand legal scrutiny. As with their judicial predecessors in the English courts, Hamilton imagines that the American version of equity would override linguistic (and even statutory) exactness in the name of fairness, drawing from traditions of mercy, conscience, and English judicial structures, even without a monarch to claim extraordinary prerogatives.

While Hamilton cites these traditions of conscience and even ideas approaching natural justice in his defense of judicial equity, one of his "Anti-Federalist" opponents raises alarms about that ancient preoccupation with statutory text and its applications. This author, going by the name Brutus, specifically frames his opposition to instituting American courts of equity through the Aristotelian lens of the intention of the law.[50] When the Constitution gives license to the judiciary to consider "all cases in law and equity," the author of *Brutus* 11 anxiously remarks that judges will be "empowered, to explain the constitution according to the reasoning spirit of it, without being confined to the words or letter."[51] By pushing beyond the constraints of the language of the law, judges will be free to impose their own rule, claiming authority under the opaque and even impressionistic notion of a "reasoning spirit."

This anxiety that the courts could work "without being confined" guides *Brutus* 11's central criticism. By invoking this "reasoning spirit," the courts—so *Brutus* 11 cautions—would emerge as uniquely powerful among the three supposedly coequal branches of government. Reiterating his calls for judicial constraints, Brutus thinks judges under the banner of equity "will not confine themselves to any fixed or established rules, but will determine, according to what appears to them, the reason and spirit" of the laws before them.[52] Echoing some of Plato's worries, Brutus thinks judges will work from hazy appearances, not steady truths. They will claim to know the "reason" of the law while only working from imprecise, unstable hunches. While earlier authors like Aristotle and Cicero might have seen the "reason and spirit" of the law as an instrument for correcting deficient statutes, Brutus instead views these notions as invitations for judicial error and even tyranny. He predicts the courts "will operate to effect, in the most certain, but yet silent and imperceptible manner," ultimately in the service of "enlarg[ing] the exercise of their powers."[53] Indeed, in his following essay, Brutus warns that "a number of clauses in the constitution, which, if explained in an equitable manner, would extend the power of the government to every case, and reduce the state legislatures to nothing."[54] For Brutus, the ancient tradition of seeking justice outside the text of the law is nothing more than a power grab by judges wielding their unchecked pretense of wisdom.

Even so, Brutus offers little in the way of an alternative to judicial discretion. Repeating some of the arguments laid out in the *Nicomachean Ethics*, he underscores how "the law, by reason of its universality, is deficient." He continues, "Since in laws all cases cannot be foreseen, or expressed, it is necessary, that when the decrees of the law cannot be applied to particular cases, there should some where be a power vested of defining those circumstances, which had they been foreseen the legislator would have expressed."[55] He even explains how the principle of equity, as Aristotle emphasizes, cannot simply be achieved with more precise and more comprehensive legislation. That is, the solution for deficient laws cannot simply be to legislate more, and as Brutus writes, "there can be no established rules and fixed principles of equity laid down, without destroying its very essence, and reducing it to a positive law."

Given Brutus's recognition of these arguments against legislative—rather than judicial—solutions for legal justice, we may not be surprised to find that Hamilton's case for the "need of the word 'equity'" ultimately won the contest for ratification. Still, what these debates of the 1770s and 1780s reveal is how both sides of this debate simply disagreed on how equity might be achieved—whether through the legislature or through the courts—and who might be counted on to pursue equity most effectively. But legal equity itself was always a goal worth pursuing. Americans fresh from the Revolutionary War were skeptical of judges issuing verdicts and determining (or perhaps imposing) a meaning of *equity* on the rest of us. Ultimately, however, the 1780s proved to be a pivotal moment in grappling with the impracticality of equity-by-legislation, leaving elite and aristocratic judges as the nation's formal institutions of conscience, fairness, and flexibility.

Democratizing Equity: The Courtroom as Classroom

As John Quincy Adams relates in his diaries (April 1829), the curriculum of Harvard College trained New England's Lowells and Thayers in the philosophers of the ancient world: "if the teacher of morals can draw no available funds from the language of Pythagoras and Plato: if the Christian Orator can draw no shaft from the quivers of Aristotle and Quintilian, or of Demosthenes and Cicero; the fault is surely not in his studies."[56] Harvard's soon-to-be justices and senators were steeped in the Greeks and Romans, and they transplanted the arguments and thoughts of these ancients into their nascent republic of the late eighteenth century.[57] Thinkers like Plato and Aristotle, however, were not champions of democracy, and the elite education afforded to students like John Quincy Adams adumbrates the aristocratic orientation of some of the framers' thinking. Indeed, in one of his most famous *Federalist* essays—*Federalist* 10, on how "to break and control the violence of faction"—James Madison cautions that "Democracies have ever been spectacles of turbulence and contention" and "have in general been as short in their lives, as they have been violent in their deaths."[58] Even with his reservations about direct democracy, Madison did not envision his "republican" form of government as something entirely undemocratic, and in the same *Federalist* essay, he carefully draws out the select "points of difference between a Democracy and a Republic," focusing on guidelines for the election of representatives.[59] The voters, Madison acknowledged, had to be counted on to have "virtue and intelligence to select men of virtue and wisdom," lest the American people find themselves governed by aristocrats rather than by themselves.[60]

These ambivalent attitudes toward democratic rule among some of America's learned and influential figures bear on our understanding of the place of legal and political equity in the first decades of America.[61] It is true that America's founders—like their ancient forebears—were wary of direct democratic control, and they incorporated aristocratic elements into the republican design of the US Constitution. But even if certain politicians today repeat the facile slogan that "America is a republic, not a democracy," there have been democratic foundations built into the structure of American political life from its very beginning. That is, America has always been both a republic *and* a democracy: as Cicero himself reminds readers in his *De Re Publica*, the republic is a mixture of democracy, aristocracy, and monarchy mixed in with a "certain degree of *aequabilitas*." The American Republic would follow Cicero's model, weaving democratic strands of equality and equity into its very fabric. Equity, in other words, would be found not just as the domain of a select coterie of judges. Ordinary, democratic citizens would have a stake in American equity too.

These other democratic institutions, well beyond the periodic election of representatives, would be connected to the principles of equity a few decades after the ratification of the Constitution by a Frenchman on tour in America. This young aristocrat, Alexis de Tocqueville, would come to publish two volumes on the democratic culture in America, touching on topics ranging from newspapers to the study of philosophy to labor relations. Alongside such democratic mores, Tocqueville also championed the role that ordinary American citizens had in achieving equity, a principle that Tocqueville—*contra* Hamilton—located outside judges' chambers. Tocqueville saw equity as the purview of democratic, not just aristocratic, actors. More particularly, Tocqueville looks to the courtroom jury as one of the key instruments for teaching the principles of equity and performing its duties, placing it in the hands of ordinary American citizens, not just those studying in the libraries surrounding Harvard Yard.

Jury trials were a part of American life since the nation's earliest days under the Constitution: the Sixth Amendment guarantees the "right to an impartial jury" in criminal cases. (The Seventh Amendment provides similar guidelines for jury trials in civil suits.) While many today see jury duty as a burden on busy schedules, Tocqueville instead sees in the jury a dignified institution that "teaches everyone that they have duties toward society and a role in its government"; moreover, by "forcing men to be concerned with affairs other than their own, this civic obligation combats individual egoism, which is to societies what rust is to metal."[62] In his eyes, the jury trial is not some matter of courtroom mechanics. It is the very schoolroom and stage of democratic citizenship. Tocqueville's admiration for democratic jury service has many elements, but one of those is his belief that the jury is where ordinary citizens, and not just the likes of Madison and Adams, can wrestle with perennial questions of justice and equity: "The jury teaches men the practice of equity (*la pratique de l'équité*). Each man, in judging his neighbor, thinks that he may in turn be judged. This is especially true of juries in civil cases. Almost no one is afraid of one day being prosecuted as a criminal, but anyone can be sued."[63]

When Tocqueville cites the "practice of equity," he underscores how jury service is something we *do*, not simply something we *study* or even *know*. To return to Myles Burnyeat's account of virtue in the *Nicomachean Ethics*, equity might be understood as the product of "our ability to internalize from a scattered range of particular cases a general evaluative attitude which is not reducible to rules or precepts."[64] In accordance with this view of equity (along with other ethical virtues), we learn to be fair and just not through the study of rarefied treatises in legal libraries but through our encounter with the "scattered range" of trials and verdicts in any American courtroom. More than just an Aristotelian ethical theorist, moreover, Tocqueville frames this training as "a certain public respect for Christian morality and equity (*un certain respect pour la morale et l'équité chrétiennes*), so that it is not easy for [Americans] to violate the laws when those laws stand in the way of their dogmas."[65] For Tocqueville, the lessons of the jury have an almost sacred valence. Our drudgery of jury duty was, in his eyes, a sacramental education in the moral conduct of democratic citizens.

Like many of the framers of the Constitution, however, Tocqueville comes from an aristocratic background, and we would be mistaken to see him as an uncomplicated champion of a kind of "common sense" equity found in all of America's unschooled democrats. He finds ordinary Americans lacking in raw intellectual power. He famously cautions against the "tyranny of the majority," the insidious psychological pressure to conform to one's fellow citizens, and he pronounces that there is "no country where there is in general less independence of mind and true freedom of discussion than in America."[66] He accuses Americans of being uninterested in books and of being monotonous and boring. It is therefore not surprising that his rosy account of the jury revolves around fundamentally aristocratic lessons that become, only circumstantially, available to those outside these upper echelons of learned society:

> The jury is incredibly useful in shaping the people's judgment and augmenting their natural enlightenment. This, in my view, is its greatest advantage. It should be seen as a free school, and one that is always open, to which each juror comes to learn about his rights, and where he enters into daily contact with the best educated, most enlightened members of the upper classes and receives practical instruction in the law in a form accessible to his intelligence.

Tocqueville leaves us with a paradox: the jury is a democratic master class in equity, but its teachers are an "enlightened" elite. Is an understanding of justice and fairness the province of "the upper classes" and the "best educated" Americans? Does Tocqueville think that, in fact, only the Lowells and Thayers grasp justice and fairness and that the rest of us learn about equity only when we are called to serve at their courthouses? With our egalitarian instincts, most Americans would bristle at Tocqueville's suggestions that only the bookish Ivy Leaguer or the moneyed entrepreneur has an authentic understanding of justice and that only through occasional conversation with them do the rest of us have any chance of grasping the same. His is an elitism that carries a whiff of Plato's proposal for clubbish philosopher-kings. It is a whiff, we shall find in the coming chapter, that lingers in the air still today.

Chapter Four

Modern Equity—Critics and Contraries

"Equity is abracadabra," snarked the English utilitarian Jeremy Bentham, calling it "a word without a meaning."[1] Writing just a few decades after the pseudonymous author of *Brutus* 11, Bentham joins a collection of critics who looked askance at the notion of equity. These detractors had their various reasons. For staunch Platonists, as we saw in the first chapter, a notion of justice that bends and adapts to the particulars of experience would fall short of an ideal, transcendental Justice-with-a-capital-J, perched atop the *Republic*'s divided line.[2] In the eighteenth and nineteenth centuries, Brutus and Bentham contended that equity would allow judges to contort the law to reach their desired results under the haughty cover of high principle. Echoing his famous rejection of natural rights as "nonsense upon stilts," Bentham presents equity as a fraudulent magical incantation—something far less substantive than his own number-crunching "hedonic calculus" that sought to provide the greatest utility to the greatest number of people.[3]

At its core, Bentham's critique rests on the accusation that equity serves as a pretense for ulterior motives. He cautions that equity's champions can define (and redefine) equity simply as "whatever has ever been done by a court of equity."[4] He views equity, then, as something not just bendable but transformable, not bound by juridical tradition but entirely absolved of real meaning. In that regard, Bentham's critique anticipates the turn of the last decade, during which equity has become a crucible of American culture wars and political polarization. As we have already seen in the Introduction, pundits on both the right and the left increasingly attack "equity initiatives" that have emerged in corporate human-resources departments, academic job advertisements, and political campaigns—and like Bentham, these critics often see equity as a deceptive cover for hidden aims. Those on the right like Christopher Rufo have presented equity in a particularly catastrophic light. He warns that "an equity-based form of government would mean the end not only of private property, but also of individual rights, equality under the law, federalism, and freedom of speech."[5] The principle of equity, he continues, is a "euphemism" to promote "critical race theory" and "identity-based Marxism."[6] Following Bentham, Rufo sees in *equity* a term that has no specific content and merely empowers political evildoers to act under its august aegis.

To be clear, I do not see Rufo as a studious descendant of Bentham. The Benthamite charge of sorcery from the bench and today's rejections of equity as a watchword of radical communism are worlds apart—they scorn equity for different reasons and, frankly, with different degrees of intellectual seriousness. We could dismiss Rufo's catastrophizing account of "identity-based Marxism" with a simple historical reality: Marx postdates Aristotle and his ancient account of legal equity by over two thousand years. It is simply untrue to call "an equity-based form of government" one opposed to the rule of law, as Aristotle's *Politics* makes clear. We could continue this litany of historical errors with Rufo's presentation of equity as something antithetical to American political thought, when Article III of the US Constitution explicitly empowers the courts to consider equity in their rulings. But enough. We should simply note that there is something ignorant, if not dishonest, about the effort to paint equity—and specifically legal equity—as some pernicious invention of Marxists and radical communists. Pundits like Rufo are welcome to go head to head with Aristotle and Hamilton, but they should stop pinning an idea they don't like on a nineteenth-century German they like even less.

Despite these historical errors, however, contemporary pundits are correct to point out that equity has become a central feature of corporate, academic, and cultural parlance in novel ways. As we have seen, search data from Google shows us that the word's use has surged in the last decade. We should at least entertain the possibility that we have conjured new definitions of equity, just as Bentham warned, that would have been unintelligible to our ancient predecessors: climate equity, racial equity, food equity, gender equity, housing equity. Are these terms merely invocations of a storied word, used to advance vanguard theories of politics and critical theory? Do contemporary calls for equity deserve skepticism not so much for being a covert Marxist revolution but instead for being meaningless? Or do these novel terms—even if never found in the texts of Aristotle, Cicero, Hamilton, and even Bentham—nonetheless stand on sturdy traditions surrounding legal interpretation, proportional equality, and governmental authority? To frame the question more directly: have those who today claim the mantle of equity—whether in matters of racial reckoning, climate activism, or urban planning—invented a concept root and branch, or does their language stem from these ancient and durable histories?

The multiple traditions we have uncovered in the preceding three chapters make this investigation more difficult than checking a dictionary for historical examples of these new terms. We should expect to find deep disagreements about the meaning of concepts like climate equity because the word *equity* itself has meant different things to different people. For those in the Aristotelian tradition, it usually denotes matters of legal flexibility, but it can also carry a meaning of dispositional mercy. In the

Ciceronian tradition, it can mean equality, proportional merit, or an attentiveness to the spirit of the law. In the Anglophone tradition, it can even refer particularly to the rulings of England's Court of Chancery. To make matters worse, the preceding chapters also show how this one concept came to our own era through at least three languages: first the Greek of the fifth and fourth centuries BCE, then the Latin of the Roman Republic, and finally the English of modern Anglophone law. And this abbreviated history leaves out the appearance of equity's cognates in Romance languages, which we encountered only briefly with Tocqueville's commentary on American juries. Today's notion of equity *isn't* radical Marxism, but it still isn't obvious what it *is*.

The task of this chapter is to take up the challenge of defining today's term and situating it in the histories of the preceding pages. Rather than give a single, unambiguous description of equity's "true meaning," I propose that there are two main intellectual strands at play in our current use of the word. To make matters more difficult, these two strands have roughly opposite meanings, making some kind of compromise or reconciliation between them impossible. As a practical recommendation, then, I propose we use the word *equity* with care, rarely by itself, and almost always with some additional element—say, a helpful adjective, an explanatory footnote. By way of conclusion, I situate the two species of equity in some twentieth-century intellectual trends: the intersectional methods of antidiscrimination legal theory and the embrace of radical subjectivity in individual psychologies. These trends help us understand the perennial difficulty of achieving equity—of each type—as we strive to promote an ethical and just society.

The Contradictions of Modern Equity

In his authoritative usage manual of modern English, the lawyer-*cum*-lexicographer Bryan Garner reports that "a surprising number of words can bear contradictory senses."[7] These so-called contronyms or autantonyms include common words like *trim*, *sanction*, and *oversight*. Just as one can trim a tablecloth by adding a decorative fringe, one can also trim the same tablecloth by taking the fringe off. Congress can approvingly sanction programs for emergency assistance after natural disasters, or it can sternly sanction countries for their violations of international treaties. We can exercise oversight by keeping a watchful eye out for intruders, or we can commit an oversight by failing to notice them slip in.

These puzzling contronyms come to us in different ways, sometimes accidents of competing etymologies as in the case of *cleave* ("to combine" but also "to separate") or accidents of competing usage as in the case of *table*, used in some places to set aside a bill and elsewhere to bring it up for debate. They are also not unique to English. One example in Latin that comes to mind is the adjective *altus*, which can either mean "high above" or "deep below." The kernel of meaning here, it would seem, is something that is vertically distant (in either direction), and as is the case with all contronyms, context usually "eliminates any real possibility of ambiguity."[8] In the sixth book of the *Aeneid*, for instance, when Aeneas descends to the underworld in search of his father, Anchises, Vergil describes the topsy-turvy geography around the River Styx and Charon's lugubrious ferry, where throngs of souls stand "thick as the leaves of the forest that at autumn's first frost drop and fall, and thick as the birds that from the seething deep (*gurgite ab alto*) flock shoreward, when the chill of the year drives them overseas and sends them into sunny lands" (6.309–312).[9] Here Vergil describes the "deep" from which sea-dwelling birds begin their migratory flight. But in the opening of the same epic, he points to the "lofty (*altae*) walls of Rome."[10] While rooted in the same concept of vertical distance, the single word ends up adopting opposite meanings just pages apart.

Latin contronyms extend beyond the imaginative depths (or heights) of Vergil's epic masterpiece. It would seem, in fact, that Cicero's *De Re Publica* and its discussions of *aequitas* provide another candidate. As we'll recall from our earlier investigation, *aequitas* to the radical democrat demands true equality (or *aequabilitas*) among citizens, whereas *aequitas* to the aristocrat rejects true equality as a failure to acknowledge distinction and status. In either of these meanings, the Latin *aequitas* aims to treat "like as like," finding some commonality within a group and determining the equal treatment for those group members. But depending on the politics of a speaker, the word can require either sameness or difference. Perhaps, though, the ambiguity surrounding *aequitas* in Cicero centers around a word that is not exactly a contronym like *trim* or *cleave*. We might say that both in the case of the aristocrat and in the case of democrat, the word carries a central meaning of equalizing the treatment of people grouped by a certain criterion, whatever that criterion may be.

The contradictory meanings of *equity* in the ancient tradition are not confined to these disagreements over proportional equality, nor are they confined to Cicero's text. Once we turn to Aristotle's consideration of legal justice, the contronym of ancient equity appears in high relief. (We don't even need to leave the Latin language when we recall that Thomas Aquinas and his followers began to use *aequitas* as an explicit translation for *epieikeia*.) This other species of equity or *aequitas*, descending from Aristotle's *epieikeia*, asks that we recognize someone as unfit for the regular application of a written law, and it demands that we treat such an outlier as a class of their own. What these ancient traditions produce—all under the same term—is, on the one hand, a principle of treating members of a group the same and, on the other hand, a principle of excusing someone from the treatment that normally applies to others.

With these opposing meanings entrenched in the centuries of equity's conceptual development, we should not be surprised today to find its clear definition always at an arm's length. In a recent study of the word's current use across political, educational, and philosophical settings, Harvard Law Professor Martha Minow underscores how "the meaning of 'equity' can be protean," especially once we leave the domains of academic study of the law and enter matters of public policy.[11] Worse than just ambiguous, *equity* and *equality*, its etymological cousin, both "may be entering the status of 'essentially contested concepts'" that "secure widespread endorsement but also expansive disagreement over their proper uses."[12] That is, people like the sound of *equity*, but no one can agree on what it actually means. Especially since Latin speakers of earlier centuries had difficulty defining *aequabilitas* and *aequitas* with any consistent specificity, it's possible we could never have avoided this confusion. In the end, Bentham might have been on to something: *equity* is not exactly "a word without a meaning," but it may well be a word without a stable, consistent, or clear one.

The term *equity* on its own, then, may be beyond rescuing, but as we have seen with Bryan Garner's collection of contronyms, words like *sanction* or *cleave* simply demand the helpful supports of context to make any sense of them. We might simply caution readers to treat the word *equity* with similar care. We might also advise writers to replace *equity* with clearer terminology, as they do with other contronyms: use *punish* for *sanction* or at least add helpful modifiers like *trim off* rather than a naked *trim*. But using *equity* unmodified places a burden on (and a hope in) the reader to elucidate a term murkier than the Styx.

One goal of my chapter here is—after mapping this linguistic morass—to offer a clear way out. Recognizing equity's status as a contronym and an "essentially contested concept," I set forth here two specific types of equity, both of which seek to advance the cause of justice but through fundamentally different, even opposite, ways. The first species I call "equity of the exception," or "exceptional equity," and it has its roots in the concept of *epieikeia* articulated in Aristotle's *Nicomachean Ethics*. The second species I call "equity of the norm," or "normalizing equity," and it stems from Cicero's discussions of *aequitas* in *De Re Publica*, which in turn takes inspiration from an earlier notion of proportional equality.

Let's look first at exceptional equity. Taking as its point of departure Aristotle's observation that statutory language will always fail to anticipate all of its idiosyncratic applications, this first kind of equity understands that we will encounter unforeseen circumstances and individuals, and therefore always using our regular rules in regular ways would amount to injustice. A Milo the wrestler, of some kind or another, will always appear. In such a case, the "equitable" person will need to bend regular protocols—just like they would bend the Lesbian leaden rule—around an exceptional case, as we saw with the medieval example of the starving traveler allowed to eat meat on Friday. Or in the spirit of Aristotle's example of the Egyptian physician who strays from standard protocols and treatments, exceptional equity recognizes that we all may find ourselves in the position of "a doctor [who] must be prepared to change" their standard treatments in the face of unexpected ailments.[13]

Contemporary examples of this brand of equity are numerous. For a blind student, a math teacher might radically alter the format of a geometry exam.[14] In the face of draconian sentencing guidelines, a judge might reduce prison terms for young criminals whose home life cultivated illegal behaviors.[15] We might imagine the admissions officer of an elite college giving extraordinary consideration to an application from a student whose rural, isolated community would have made access to extracurricular activities and required tests impossible. In all these cases, these practitioners have the opportunity to alter their standard practices and rules to accommodate the exceptional and unexpected particulars of cases before them. And at least in Aristotle's view, to cling to standard protocols in such situations would amount to an unethical punctiliousness.

As our ancient sources highlight again and again, one key element of this equity of the exception is the unanticipated nature of extraordinary cases. Martha Minow echoes these historical accounts in her survey of contemporary views of equity. Today the "results [of equitable interpretation] can be unpredictable, subject to the views or whims of particular decision-makers."[16] But as we see above, physicians, academics, and jurists sometimes need to exercise their own prudential judgment, even against the strict demands of standard practice, to do what is right. Minow's characterization of this decision-making process as one rooted in "whims" might suggest to some that exceptional equity is a matter of sheer arbitrariness or caprice. Even in the ancient tradition, this is not the case. For Aristotle, the ability to make reasoned choices, particularly when we cannot resort to mechanical rules, underlies his notion of *phronēsis*, a word that Latin writers would later call *prudentia*, itself a compressed form of the noun *providentia*.[17] Such choices, in other words, demand "prudential" judgments rather than mechanical formulas; thus, equity of the exception asks us to make nonobvious decisions about nonobvious cases. In this view, we occasionally need to abandon meticulous rule-following, no matter how noble our mission statements and sentencing guidelines may be, because rules alone can never make a just world. We should not, therefore, identify bureaucratic fealty to "best practices" with the pursuit of justice, which sometimes demands unpredictable, but ultimately prudential, disobedience.

The second species of equity comes to the fore in Cicero's *De Re Publica*. I call this second type normalizing equity, or equity of the norm—that which locates a commonality within a group of people according to which we can justify equal treatment of that group's members. Anticipating the Latin tradition from which we get our term *equity*, Aristotle calls this principle "proportional equality," which demands that we treat "like as like." In the pursuit of this second kind of equity, we might look for people who are treated differently despite being equal members of the same group and try to rectify their erroneously disparate conditions. In this sense, normalizing equity is the reverse of exceptional equity in that it aims to draw out and act on commonalities rather than isolating an exception and justifying nonstandard treatment.

The criteria by which we define these groups, of course, can take different forms. According to the aristocratic view presented in *De Re Publica*, equity of the norm justifies a stratification of society: The aristocrat claims that their class deserves more rights than those in subordinate classes. But equity of norm need not just be about assigning special privileges; we might also view proportional equality as an invitation to prop up those whose common trait is a burden they bear. An example of this approach underlies the well-known, ironic adage from Anatole France's *The Red Lily*: "The law, in its majestic equality, forbids the rich as well as the poor to sleep under bridges, to bed in the streets, and to steal bread." In France's view, those who are rich and poor constitute two separate groups who deserve two different standards or norms of fairness. Those who are poor merit their own kind of treatment—one that offers support and mercy—on account of their shared hardships. As a counterweight to Cicero's aristocratic spokesman, *The Red Lily* bitingly underscores how those who are destitute belong to a special class that demands different treatment—that is, some measure of charity—in the name of justice.

Generally, this second kind of equity strives to produce a shared outcome appropriate to all members of a group. In her aforementioned study of equity in contemporary legal theory, Martha Minow shows how contemporary advocates of equity sometimes situate their pursuit of justice in such a frame. These advocates reject a "particularized conception of justice focused on what each person deserves"—that is, a conception attentive to individual difference.[18] Instead, they call "for changing systems to produce something approximating equality of outcomes for groups defined along certain dimensions—chiefly race."[19] These groups, however we might define them, include members whose shared trait merits equal treatment among themselves but not with members outside that group, for this kind of equity "demands attention and responses to different starting points, systemic disadvantages, and conditions affecting" the ultimate standing of the group.[20] Others are even more explicit that this second kind of equity should strive for "equality of outcomes for groups defined along certain dimensions."[21]

As Minow's article helpfully draws out, both species of equity can be found in contemporary society, and equity's champions use the same word to denote these two opposite goals. Equity's doppelgänger scenario is no historical accident, nor is it a fault of contemporary linguistic sloppiness. Those who advance equity of whichever kind have inherited these divisive, and indeed divided, concepts, all transmitted under the same lexicographical heading from two strands of thought in the ancient world. In the name of literary economy, many will continue to use the naked term *equity* as a rallying cry for justice, but with that word standing on its own, we may well not grasp the cause for which they are fighting.

At the Intersections of Equity—A Contemporary Exploration of Normalizing Equity

Central to Plato's ideal state in his *Republic* is a rigid stratification of the population into three separate groups: the wise philosophers, the courageous soldiers, and the productive craftsmen. Carefully sorted into their roles through the city's education system, the citizens of the *kallipolis* are, on the one hand, seen as equal members of the city but, on the other hand, considered fundamentally different from those outside their groups. "Meddling and exchange among these three classes," Socrates warns, "is the greatest harm that can happen to the city and would rightly be called the worst evil."[22] Even if Plato presents these classes as three communities mutually necessary to the well-being of his city, he nevertheless positions the philosophers as the best of the bunch. According to Socrates's "noble lie" used to justify these castes—that people are born with a certain "metallic" character—philosophers deserve to rule on account of their golden souls, and likewise soldiers take their position because of their silver souls. Those sorted into the bronze class of manual laborers are immovably stationed in their lowest (but still, somehow, equal) role.

Students are often appalled by Plato's proposal, suspicious of the elite philosophers who peer into the souls of other citizens in order to slot them into rigid social roles—and who conveniently set themselves at the top of Plato's civic ladder. Alongside these suspicions, undergraduates in the liberal arts are doubly critical of Plato since they themselves are told that their pursuit of intellectual life at the university is compatible with, even conducive to, successful careers in business, engineering, and other "productive" occupations. French poetry, we say, will make them better energy analysts. Americans more broadly also champion a belief in social mobility, a concept at odds with Plato's rigid castes. And perhaps most fundamentally of all, modern readers of Plato usually reject the view that their individuality—a complex amalgam of ethnicity, sexual orientation, religion, musical preferences, athletic habits, and so on—could dissolve under Plato's tripartite social blueprint.

Plato was not the only author to assign citizens to rigid strata. Aristotle notoriously sets out a theory of "natural slavery" in the first book of his *Politics*, and Cicero's *De Re Publica* similarly entertains the idea of a formal aristocracy. These texts all revolve around a set of related questions. Is there such a thing as an elite, and what specifically sets them apart from the rest of us? Do some people deserve special political and civil authority on account of their aristocratic status? Should democracies treat all citizens identically? And can they do so without erasing the individual histories and characters of each citizen? Central not just to ancient thinkers, these questions motivated the French Revolution and Mao's Cultural Revolution, and they even sit at the center of contemporary discussions of wealth inequality and human rights.

Perhaps the most fraught of such sociological groupings in American culture today is categorization according to race—it is a categorization that suffuses our country's history, its policy decisions, and even its geography. Of course, a comprehensive study of race in American life is well beyond the scope of this book, but as we have already seen above in Martha Minow's account of equity and equality, race is often taken as a springboard for contemporary discussions of these terms. In what ways do groupings along matters of race reveal unjust aspects of modern life? To what extent should racial equality—alongside other matters like sex equality, environmental stewardship, and so on—serve as our barometer for our society's achievement of equity, justice, and even virtue?

In a landmark 1989 article, "Demarginalizing the Intersection of Race and Sex: A Black Feminist Critique of Antidiscrimination Doctrine, Feminist Theory, and Antiracist Politics," Columbia Law School Professor Kimberlé Crenshaw sets out a novel framework for answering these questions. By exposing "a problematic consequence of the tendency to treat race and gender as mutually exclusive categories of experience and analysis," Crenshaw urges her readers instead to view such categories as overlapping and even compounding in their discriminatory effects.[23] Crenshaw's multidimensional approach to antidiscrimination, known as *intersectionality*, is best seen through a concrete example. She underscores how *women* or *African Americans* as groupings are themselves insufficient for understanding the experiences of those who fall under both. "With Black women as the starting point," she writes, "it becomes more apparent how dominant conceptions of discrimination condition us to think about subordination as disadvantage occurring along a single categorical axis."[24] In other words, discrimination protections might fail to achieve their goals when Black women are treated strictly as women or strictly as African Americans but not both simultaneously. Crenshaw cites an employment discrimination lawsuit where the plaintiffs brought "a suit not on behalf of Blacks or women, but specifically on behalf of Black women."[25] Summarizing the court's rejection of the suit's central contention, Crenshaw observes how "Black women are protected only to the extent that their experiences coincide with those of either" Black men or white women.[26] But at least in this particular ruling, the discrimination against Black women—understood as a meaningful category unto itself—was left unrecognized and unremedied.

Even if Crenshaw's article focuses on contemporary American discrimination law, it nevertheless grows out of some perennial concerns we have seen in the preceding chapters, especially as they bear on matters of normalizing equity. This species of equity asks us to treat like as like: members of a group, however that group is defined, deserve to be treated similarly. Unlawful discrimination violates these norms. According to Crenshaw's intersectional example above, we might find that Blacks are treated like other racial groups and that women are treated like men, but these categories belie how the legal guarantees accorded to all people are not accorded to Black women. Even when we claim to treat like as like, these more granular, complex subgroups reveal how we fall short. Our Venn diagram of equity—with its overlapping demographic circles—must always attend to its intersecting areas in the name of ensuring proportional justice for every inch of its ethical geometry.

Crenshaw's intersectional approach here is not limited to matters of race, and in an interview considering the decades-long legacy of her article's publication, she notes that it applies to matters of class, sexual orientation, and other social and legal categories.[27] We might extend her compounding dimensions of injustice to matters such as age, geographical origin, political party, occupation, and whatever other matters people use to define their own characters and that others use to view (and possibly discriminate against) them. Our Venn diagram with all its intersecting subgroups can become complicated, even overwhelmingly so. Indeed, demographic qualities and their combinations are practically as innumerable as the people on the planet. Taken to its logical endpoint, intersectionality reminds us of the infinitely rich and unique lived experiences we should consider in our efforts to become more just.

Seen through the visual metaphor of intersecting lines or overlapping circles, Crenshaw's approach rebuts some of the tenets of the *Republic*'s social stratification. Plato identifies strictly three categories of citizens, but Crenshaw's various demographic categories create dozens. Plato contends that "meddling and exchange" of a city's classes spell civic disaster, but Crenshaw demands our increased attention to demographic combinations that we ought to recognize separately. Plato insists that his three castes can all enjoy equal standing as citizens of the *kallipolis*, but Crenshaw warns that intersectional, overlapping categorization jeopardizes true civic equality. By multiplying her vast permutations of humanity, Crenshaw's intersectionality highlights how treating like as like becomes all the more difficult when demographic categories become compound, complex, and even countless.

These difficulties magnify the philosophical paradoxes that Aristotle highlighted millennia ago surrounding the rule of law, equality, and even ethics more broadly. As he cautions in the opening book of the *Nicomachean Ethics*, matters like politics and ethical philosophy are imprecise sciences, and they always "involve great variation and irregularity."[28] To demand that individuals be reducible to a single "categorical axis"— one defined strictly by race or religion, for example—flattens the multidimensional character of human beings. We are all, indeed, more "variable" and "irregular" than one demographic checkbox, and Crenshaw's productive legal framework exposes how this complexity can inspire equally complicated miscarriages of justice. More straightforwardly, intersectionality resuscitates and enriches the questions of proportional equality. Can we claim to treat "like as like" when we group people by one trait alone? In what ways does "equity of the norm" inevitably elide the intersectional identities of particular humans? With whom, among the world's remarkable diversity of people, should we be collected into a group, and for what reasons? Understood through the lens of "equity of the norm," Crenshaw gives a name to those misgivings many have about Plato's tripartite castes in his ideal city. Recognizing that no one could be *merely* a craftsman or *merely* a courageous soldier, we today might also recognize that no one is *merely* a member of their sex or *merely* a member of their racial group.

Others have taken their frustration with demographic categories—no matter how precise, scientific, or intersectional—as the point of departure for criticizing such groupings entirely. One example of this alternative approach sits at the heart of *The Omni-Americans*, a 1970 book by essayist, novelist, and co-founder of Jazz at Lincoln Center Albert Murray. The subtitle of Murray's book takes aim at the "Folklore of White Supremacy," and in some ways, it anticipates Crenshaw's critique of reductive racial categories. But instead of asking his readers to attend to overlapping dimensions of demographic and legal classification, Murray instead focuses on the deficiency of any and all groupings to capture the diversity and creativity of Black American life:

> [S]o barbarous is the anthropological value system to which contemporary American social science seems to be geared that so far as the technicians who survey Negro communities are concerned, people without affluence and power are only creature-like beings whose humanity is measured in terms of their potential to accumulate material goods and exercise force with arrogance.
>
> Alas, not even the most fundamental human value that democratic societies are specifically designed to guarantee seems to count for very much once such technicians become involved with Negroes. On the contrary, far from revealing any significant preoccupation with or even appreciation for personal freedom and self-realization in any intrinsic sense, the technicians now proceed in an alarming number of instances as if statistical measurements of central tendencies . . . have become a means of justifying an ever-increasing standardization, regimentation, and conformity. In so doing, they tend to condemn the very elements in U.S. Negro life style that other non-totalitarian cultures seek and celebrate: its orientation to elastic individuality, for one, and its esthetic receptivity, and its unique blend of warmth, sensitivity, nonsense, vitality, and elegance.[29]

Of course, Murray is writing social criticism, not academic scholarship, and his critique here of "American social science" and its "technicians" does not exactly apply to legal theorists like Crenshaw reframing the historical paradigms of race-based discrimination. Even so, Murray's approach stands as a fundamental challenge to efforts at ever refining normalizing equity. Specifically, he attacks technicians and statistical demographers as false allies of Black Americans. By measuring the position of Black Americans by "their potential to accumulate material goods," such social scientists overlook the "elastic individuality" that Murray takes to be modern democracy's source of "vitality." He glorifies the eccentric, the unclassifiable, the exception.

Perhaps most important is Murray's valorization of "nonsense." As we learned in the first chapter, Aristotle rejects mathematical predictability and precision in human living, and political life demands a looseness not found in the laws of geometry and physics. Murray would seem amenable to this viewpoint. In his eyes, we should embrace a view of human culture that produces the strange and unpredictable. We should celebrate Milo the wrestler and design our society's rules to accommodate him. For Murray and others, as we shall see next, "personal freedom and self-realization" emerge as the height of human achievement, and we should welcome the opportunity to bend our laws of equity around those exceptions whom—luckily for us—we never saw coming.

We Are All Exceptions

Our earliest Greek poetry is also some of the longest: thick volumes of Homeric epic about the death of Patroclus and the spousal steadfastness of Penelope. These poems—the *Iliad* and the *Odyssey*—offer a glimpse of how the Greeks began to see themselves as a people against the backdrop of a larger (and mythical) Mediterranean world. Sometimes these poems showcase how different the Greeks are from their "barbaric" neighbors, as when the one-eyed Polyphemus devours Odysseus's comrades trapped in his cave. Elsewhere, Homer puts common humanity on display, as when Achilles, sympathetic to Trojan tragedy, delivers the corpse of his nemesis Hector to his inconsolable father. These epics set the boundaries for the Greeks' own conception of their similarities and differences among the peoples around them: to whom are they equals, and from whom are they separate? With whom should they be "normalized"?

Not all early Greek poetry privileges these civilizational, categorizing questions. Writing shortly after Homer's poems were finally put to paper, a renowned poet on the island of Lesbos—Sappho—wrote lyric poems about her own loves, her own sorrows, and her own moments. Of such high repute in the ancient world was Sappho that she was called the "Tenth Muse," and her intricate meters were copied by scores of later poets, including Romans like Catullus and Horace. On the scraps of dirty papyrus on which much of her poetry survives, Sappho tells us about the scents of violets, the setting of the moon, the texture of a girlfriend's hair. In one of her longer fragments, she tells us how she prefers these intimate topics and how the martial narratives of Homer's poetry carry little interest for her: "Some men say an army of horse and some men say an army on foot and some men say an army of ships is the most beautiful thing on the black earth. But I say it is what you love."[30]

For Sappho, Hector's "army of horse" or Agamemnon's "army of ships" isn't beautiful or perhaps even impressive. Instead, the "most beautiful thing on the black earth" is whatever—or whomever—we happen to love. Embracing a principle of radical subjectivity, Sappho sympathizes with Helen of Troy in the same poem and justifies her abrupt departure from Greece: "Not for her children nor for her dear parents had she a thought." Helen's family, her homeland, those armies of ships and horses could hold no sway over her after she fell in love with the Trojan prince Paris.[31] And whether others shared that love is entirely irrelevant to the power and validity of Helen's own desires. She is her own person. Her psychology belongs only to her.

In a way, Sappho anticipates Albert Murray when he praises "elastic individuality" insofar as his term covers our subjective preferences and identities, perhaps hinted at in *The Omni-Americans*'s nod to "esthetic receptivity" and even "nonsense." Both Sappho and Murray find value in the unique and errant. In the two millennia between these authors, others have taken up the defense of similar notions of radical subjectivity and individual psychology. In the twentieth century, perhaps the greatest champion of this frame was Sigmund Freud, who lamented the irreconcilable conflict between our idiosyncratic inner lives and the conformist demands of any human society:

> Just as a planet revolves around a central body as well as rotating on its own axis, so the human individual takes part in the course of development of mankind at the same time as he pursues his own path in life. But to our dull eyes the play of forces in the heavens seems fixed in a never-changing order; in the field of organic life we can still see how the forces contend with one another, and how the effects of the conflict are continually changing. So, also, the urges, the one towards personal happiness and the other towards union with other human beings, must struggle with each other in every individual; and so, also, the two processes of individual and of cultural development must stand in hostile opposition to each other and mutually dispute the ground.[32]

For Sappho, Freud, and Murray, a broader civilization or culture is the backdrop against which the individual must struggle to find room for their own "personal freedom and self-realization," as Murray puts it. To demand conformity, to achieve "normalization," even to group people along any dimension amounts to an unjust quashing of the irreducible individual. These authors press us to recognize and celebrate our universal exceptionalism, whether in Sapphic subjectivity, Freudian "personal happiness," or Murray's "elastic individuality."

I want to pause on Murray's notion of the elastic character of the individual. Speaking about the person and not the law, Murray's choice of words here nevertheless reminds us of Aristotle's original leaden rule, bending around the unpredicted and unpredictable. Just as the Egyptian doctor of the *Politics* needs to tailor his standard protocols to the medical anomaly, Murray rejects the statistician's ardent efforts to regularize and normalize. They all, in short, remind us of the tension between the universal rule and the individual case, between the rigidity of the law and the singularity of the person. From Sappho to Murray, they are all, to varying degrees, champions of diversity.

What earlier in this chapter I called *equity of the exception* we might instead call *accommodation of the singular*, and all these authors in their own way make their case for a practice in that vein.[33] The ways in which, the degree to which, and the reasons for which we might treat someone as an exception are difficult to pin down—indeed, that is Aristotle's central point against mechanical, mathematical ethics. Writing in the final decades of the twentieth century and in Freud's shadow, the philosopher Richard Rorty offers some guidance on how we might proceed.[34] He similarly embraces human subjectivity, and he doubts we could find a single "human community" with "recognition of a core self, the human essence, in all human beings."[35] As an inversion of the Platonist search for transcendental universals, Rorty instead wants to locate human community in our own efforts "to see more and more traditional differences (of tribe, religion, race, customs, and the like) as unimportant when compared with similarities with respect to pain and humiliation—the ability to think of people wildly different from ourselves as included in the range of 'us.'"[36] To that end, he urges us "to *create* a more expansive sense of solidarity than we presently have. The wrong way is to think of it as urging us to *recognize* such a solidarity, as something that exists antecedently to our recognition of it."[37] In short, Rorty wants us to stop searching for some preexisting common criterion that we all share as members of the same group of humans. The burden is on us to fashion such a criterion ourselves, "to see other human beings as 'one of us' rather than as 'them' [through] a matter of detailed description of what unfamiliar people are like and of redescription of what we ourselves are like."[38]

If our commonality with others—even our shared humanity—is always a matter of manufacture, always a matter of revision, always a matter of "redescription," we should not be surprised to find people who sit outside the bounds of our expectations and preexisting rules. Each of us is unique, exceptional, incommensurable. Our rules will continually fail to anticipate humanity's infinite diversity. In order to better understand our heretofore unencountered exceptions, Rorty contends that we must embrace the particular and give up on theoretical universals. This learning comes through "genres such as ethnography, the journalist's report, the comic book, the docudrama, and, especially, the novel," all as part of "a general turn against theory and toward narrative."[39] Rorty urges us to turn to literature—novels, television shows, plays, movies, and other formats—to refine our awareness and sensitivity to the edge cases we have never encountered and could never imagine on our own. This education in narrative, too, might expose how our own categories of race, religion, sex, and humanity itself are imperfect and therefore worthy of bending. Especially when we consider equity of the exception, which entails recognizing difference and judging how (and how much) our regular rules should apply, Rorty gives us clear direction: put down our Plato and dust off our Dickens.

In our final chapter, we consider Rorty's recommended curriculum. How do we learn the right ways to group humans? How can we recognize deserving outliers—those hungry wrestlers deserving of extraordinary treatment? As Aristotle tells us in the *Nicomachean Ethics*, we learn how to measure the length of the leaden rule in our geometry class, but to learn why and how much to bend it is a different sort of learning altogether. In other words, we need to attend to the real problem—recognized from Greek antiquity and still unresolved in Rorty's writings—of equitable education. We need to learn not just how to teach equitably but also how to teach equity. As with the concept of *epieikeia* itself, the question of how to teach equitable judgment and ethical virtue more generally is one of the oldest in Western philosophy, and it is the question to which we now turn.

Chapter Five

Learning to Be Fair

About a decade after the terrors of the First World War, the American classicist Edith Hamilton called fifth-century Athens "the rarest of achievements."[1] Her hagiographic account of the Athenians' "flowering of genius" in *The Greek Way* could be read as her own nostalgia for a more peaceful past, one in stark contrast with the transatlantic anguish of those war-torn decades a century ago. There was, indeed, a period during which the Athenians touted their own classical greatness, which they achieved after fighting back Persian aggression. After the Battles of Marathon and Salamis, the triumphant Athenians augmented both their self-image and their coffers, much of their money collected in the name of mutual defense from their numerous Hellenic allies. By funneling funds from these associated Greek city-states into Athens, the *polis* found itself newly enriched and confident and finally without the distraction of Persian armies. Critics today might rankle at Hamilton's near-fawning admiration of Greek culture, but at least in the cold calculus of geopolitical dominance, its achievements were indeed rare and decisive.

Athens was eager to trumpet its power. According to the historian Thucydides, the Athenians' military and civic leader Pericles proclaimed in 431 BCE that their city was "rather a pattern to others than imitators ourselves."[2] Pericles was speaking of the Athenians' constitution and political traditions, but he might as well have been talking about their artistic achievements. Their newfound wealth ushered in bold creativity in the material arts: the towering columns of the *Parthenon*, the balanced *contrapposto* in the *Doryphoros* of Polykleitos, the kinetic contours of Myron's *Discobolos*. In the dramatic arts, too, the Athenians began experimenting with works like Aeschylus's *Agamemnon* and Sophocles's *Antigone*. In her reverential assessment, Hamilton concludes that "in all Greek art" there is an achievement that "the world has yet to see again."[3]

Even Hamilton, however, would have to admit that this Athenian cultural apex was short-lived. One year after his patriotic boasting, Pericles would die during an epidemic that brought the "awful spectacle of men dying like sheep."[4] A few decades later, the Athenians would suffer humiliating self-sabotage in the Peloponnesian War, falling to their Spartan neighbors at the end of the fifth century. The aftermath of this collapse brought about tectonic changes for Athens, which was taken over by Sparta-appointed oligarchs and shortly thereafter subjugated by Philip II of Macedon, the father of Alexander the Great. In the midst of this disorienting decline, Athenian intellectuals—in a way, anticipating Hamilton—grappled with their civic malaise. Could the Athenians have avoided defeat? What kind of constitution could have flourished or at least persisted throughout these tumultuous decades? How could citizens be trained to preserve a more robust, more prosperous, more durable *polis*?

Foremost among these thinkers was Plato, himself a bitter critic of Athenian democracy. But he was not the only one who addressed these questions during this difficult period. Perhaps Plato's most prominent rival was Isocrates, who also "sought to compensate for the lack of enlightened statesmanship and mindful citizenship apparent throughout Hellas in the aftermath of the Peloponnesian War."[5] Isocrates, however, had no patience for Plato's intellectualized methods and idealized *kallipolis*, the utopia he sketched in the *Republic*. He rails against those who focus on "wonder-workings, which provide no benefit but attract crowds of the ignorant."[6] Setting those he reviles as a foil for his own brass-tacks mindset, Isocrates advises that "those wishing to do something useful must rid all their activities of pointless discourse and irrelevant action."[7] Isocrates urgently wanted his state again to be "a pattern to others."

We should not, however, take Isocrates for an uncurious politico. Like Plato and Aristotle, Isocrates sees political problems in large part as educational problems, and like them, he develops his own sophisticated framework of civic education, designed to uplift the citizens of a wounded Athens. Most important for our study here, one key element of that framework is *epieikeia*, the same word that would later come to mean *legal equity* in Aristotle's *Nicomachean Ethics* and that would spawn a millennia-long tradition of thinking about fairness, equality, and ethical virtue more broadly. At least in Isocrates's eyes, civic education and political renewal demand that students be taught to understand and strive for equity, which in turn is fundamental to a citizen's ability to make themselves useful to their city. Writing against the backdrop of the Athenians' desperate attempts to reinvigorate their faltering, fractured politics, Isocrates shows us what equity-based education might look like and why a civic-minded culture like postwar Athens would be eager—desperate, even—to cultivate it.

Isocrates's Workhorse "Philosophy"

In the ninth book of the *Iliad*, the tutor Phoenix tells Achilles that he was entrusted to turn the precocious solider into a "speaker of words and a doer of deeds."[8] Ever since Phoenix's struggle to tame his swift-footed student, the Greeks have wrestled with the problem of how, what, and even why to teach their young. Before Isocrates's birth in the second half of the fifth century, these educational matters erupted into a cultural controversy with the rise of the so-called sophists, who traveled from city to city offering their intellect in exchange for pay. Drawn from the same word *sophia* ("wisdom") found in the Greek word *philosophia* ("love of wisdom"), the epithet sophist often meant something more like "wise guy" than "wise man." To some, they were simply in the business of teaching the young, but to many, sophists were bookish charlatans. The earliest and possibly most notorious of these sophists was the relativist Protagoras, who pronounced, "Man is the measure of all things." Another sophist we have already encountered is Thrasymachus, who, in the opening of Plato's *Republic*, anticipates Machiavellian politicking by arguing that justice is merely "the advantage of the stronger." Depending on your philosophical views, sophists like Protagoras and Thrasymachus could be fearless truth-tellers or destructive nihilists. Perhaps both.

In light of the sophists' besmirched reputation, Isocrates tries to distance himself from them. In fact, he composed an early treatise called *Against the Sophists* with this very goal in mind, written around 390. Near the end of that text, Isocrates reinforces that one of the sophists' most famous claims—that ethical virtue could be taught—is not part of his own educational program: "Let no one think that I mean that a sense of justice is teachable. I contend that there is no sort of art that can convert those who by nature lack virtue to soundness of mind and a sense of justice."[9] Leaning into an idea of in-born "talent" that one needs to be a good person, Isocrates tries to moderate expectations for his teaching abilities. He can only refine the good nature that is already found in capable students, and "the study of political speeches can assist in encouraging and training these faculties."[10] He cannot turn coal into a diamond, but he can expertly polish the uncut gems under his tutelage.

As Isocrates hints in the brief statements above, this "encouraging and training" is not like the philosophical regimen we find in Plato. When he writes that he wants to lead students to "soundness of mind and a sense of justice," he tells us they can reach these goals through the "study of political speeches," not by the arduous epistemological ascent up the divided line. Even so, Isocrates wants us to take him as a serious and profound thinker, and he repeatedly remarks that his educational program is one rooted in philosophy, or *philosophia*, the same "love of wisdom" that we apply to the dialogues of Plato and the schemata of Aristotle. Immediately before his denial that one could ever teach a "sense of justice," in fact, Isocrates distills his overall aim in language now familiar to us: "those who wish to follow the prescriptions of my philosophy (*philosophia*) may be helped more quickly to reasonableness (*epieikeia*) than to speechmaking."[11]

Before we jump to what Isocrates means here by positioning reasonableness, or *epieikeia*, as his ultimate goal, it's important for us to understand how his notion of philosophy is radically different from that shared by many of the thinkers featured in the preceding pages of this book. Isocrates does not want to be seen as a mere speech coach, one who teaches his students the slick-talking trickery of the salesperson, but he also doesn't want to be taken for another Plato. He contends that—in the face of widespread misunderstanding by rival intellectual figures—he alone has the correct view of philosophy.

Near the end of his *Antidosis*, a defense of his teaching modeled on the *Apology* of Socrates, Isocrates tells us about his unique brand of philosophy: "what some people call *philosophia* is not really that at all."[12] He tells us that those who are truly "wise (*sophoi*) are those who have the ability to reach the best opinions (*doxai*) most of the time, and philosophers (*philosophoi*) are those who spend time acquiring such an intelligence as quickly as possible."[13] His comments here amount to a critique of intellectuals like Plato and Socrates: those overly theoretical, head-in-the-clouds thinkers whose discussions about the parts of the soul or the divided line don't address the pressing problems of the day. We might hear Isocrates speaking in the voice of an anxious parent steering their child away from a philosophy major—"How will you ever get a job with that?"—as he stresses efficiency, applicability, and relevancy. His students will reach the "best opinions," or *doxai*, even if they never grasp transcendental truths. They will succeed "most of the time," even if they sometimes come up short. As a forerunner of office managers (and academic advisers, speaking as one myself), Isocrates is happy to remind us that done is better than perfect.

With this "close enough to get the job done" approach to *philosophia*, it's tempting to read Isocratean *epieikeia* as a rough equivalent to Aristotle's equity of the exception. Both abandon strict rule-following. And like Aristotle's later recommendations to bend the law around extraordinary cases, Isocrates's principle here also draws from the etymological roots of *epieikeia*, meaning something like "according to what is apparent" or "regarding what is suitable." Indeed, Isocrates wants us to attend to "apparent" problems with "suitable" solutions. But there are fundamental differences between the two thinkers. Aristotle, we will recall, wants us to bend the law around the rare outlier by excavating the intent of legislators and preserving the regular rule of law by acknowledging how language can sometimes come up short in its static formulations. Isocratean *epieikeia*, however, is not built on reverence for legal regularity. It instead constitutes permission to engage in ideological shape-shifting in the service of practical results. We might translate it as *adaptability*, *spontaneity*, or even *license*.

Indeed, *Against the Sophists* encourages its readers to abandon standard rules entirely, not just making occasional and unforeseen exceptions in applying the laws. For Isocrates, standard, rule-bound procedures are crutches for the uncreative spirit, and he finds the true "philosopher"—the one most attuned to "reasonableness"—in the individual who can pursue novel, *ad hoc* solutions at every turn: "What is said by one person is not useful in a similar way for the next speaker, but that man seems most skillful who both speaks worthily of the subject matter and can discover things to say that are entirely different from what others have said.... Speeches cannot be good unless they reflect the circumstances (*kairoi*), propriety (*to prepon*), and originality."[14]

Here Isocrates trots out terms that Athenians would recognize as elements of political speech-making. *Kairoi* can refer to "that which is appropriate to (or needful in) the circumstances," or it can simply mean "advantage."[15] The notion of the *prepon*, or the "fitting," too, has a profound and durable influence on all sorts of political and legal orators in the Greek and Roman periods.[16] In the end, the immutable forms of Plato are just as antithetical to Isocrates's program as stock phrases and formulaic arguments: the true Isocratean "philosopher" is the one who can "discover things to say that are entirely different from what others have said." Seen through this lens, Isocratean *epieikeia* entails an eager malleability to adapt to all the demands of the moment—any moment.

Other works build on Isocrates's vision of training students to look to the "suitable" as their guiding philosophical principle, often returning to the specific language of *epieikeia*. In his *Encomium of Helen*, which begins with a summary of his methods and his opposition to other philosophical educators, Isocrates advertises his pragmatic bent and slanders the "hairsplitting" nonsense of heady Athenian intellectuals. They

> should throw away this hairsplitting, which pretends to make refutations in speech but which has long since been refuted in action. They should pursue truth, educate their students about the affairs in which we act as citizens, and develop their

students' experience of these matters, with the consideration that it is much better to conjecture reasonably (*epieikōs*) about useful things than to know precisely (*akribōs*) what is useless, and that to be a little ahead in important matters is better than to excel in small matters that are no help in life.[17]

If others pursue "speech," Isocrates pursues "action." When Isocrates pursues the "truth," it is a truth grounded in the practical demands of citizen life. His education program aims to produce assiduous, pragmatic students who can "conjecture reasonably (*epieikōs*) about useful things." They may not have "precise" knowledge, but their knowledge will be good enough, and better yet, it will be good enough for those "important matters" that advance the interests of the vulnerable Athenian state. All these recommendations, as he put it in *Against the Sophists*, are in service of preparing students "more quickly to *epieikeia*." Above all else, they will be "reasonable."

What does this really mean, to be "reasonable"? What are reasonable actions, and what does it mean to "conjecture reasonably"? Revisiting Aristotle is again helpful for drawing out Isocrates's particular vision. On the one hand, it is true that Aristotle and Isocrates share the same suspicions about stable, inflexible notions of Platonic justice. Students shouldn't worry about "hairsplitting" arguments that get bogged down arguing "precisely (*akribōs*)" and should instead "conjecture reasonably (*epieikōs*)" about "important matters" that demand speedy attention. Foreshadowing Aristotle's own claim that "it is a mark of an educated person to look for precision (*akribeia*) in each kind of inquiry just to the extent that the nature of the subject allows it," Isocrates urges us to stop worrying about precise, intellectual arguments when we have a city to run and a citizenry to educate.[18] Others have written about how "Aristotle's close encounters with the school of Isocrates . . . seem to have left a mark," and their shared embrace of "imprecision" in political matters shows us how their affinity extends beyond the occasional shared word.[19]

The similarities between Aristotle and Isocrates, however, are limited. Aristotle, perhaps more than Plato, could be seen as the most "hairsplitting" of all the Greek philosophers, with his careful categorization of voluntary actions in the *Nicomachean Ethics* and his endless taxonomies of sea creatures in his *History of Animals*. And even if both Aristotle and Isocrates laud *epieikeia* as the proper principle for guiding our imprecise politics, they understand the term in rather different ways. We should again recall that Aristotle's treatment of *epieikeia* is specifically a matter of legal justice, and he deploys that principle for the sake of "exceptional equity," bending mechanical rules in a "reasonable" way around exceptional cases. In the *Ethics*, he sketches "who the reasonable person (*epieikēs*) is: the sort who decides on and does things of this kind, and who is not a stickler for justice in the bad sense but rather tends to take a less strict view of things."[20] In contrast to Isocrates's dogged pursuit of "useful things," "important matters," and "advantage" through training in *epieikeia*, Aristotle deploys this principle as part of his project of fostering the "general evaluative attitude" whereby students learn how to pursue the "noble and the just."[21] In short, Aristotle urges students to follow *epieikeia* in order to do *good*, not just in order to do *well* for themselves.

Especially when we find that Aristotle's aspiration is not simply to win an office or become a democratic celebrity but instead to approximate "the activity of a god, superior as it is in blessedness, [since it is] one of reflection," we imagine that Isocrates would not hesitate to call these Aristotelian objectives "wonder-workings" best abandoned in the service of political urgency.[22] Blessedness does not pay off government debt, nor does it defeat hostile armies. Indeed, scholars observe that "traits that appear as moral defects to Aristotle appear fairly often as virtues in Isocrates," and their shared terminology nevertheless leads them to opposite ends.[23] While both Aristotle and Isocrates see *epieikeia* or reasonableness or equity as a laudable principle, they conceive of the term in fundamentally different ways. For Aristotle, the equitable is the just "and better than just in one sense."[24] Later thinkers followed this highminded view. For Anglophone jurists like Lord Ellesmere at the Court of Chancery, "law and equity . . . both aim at one and the same end, which is to do right." Alexander Hamilton in *Federalist* 80, too, underscores that "equity would not tolerate" what is "unconscionable" in a society. Whether in equity of the exception or in equity of the norm, these concepts demand a certain degree of idealism: that the world could be made better somehow, and we should strive for those improvements. For Isocrates, however, equity is getting one's head out of the books and approaching problems with expedient cunning.[25] If his equity is a Benthamite "abracadabra," he conjures not justice but results.

In sum, these passages sketch how Isocrates aligned *epieikeia* with the immediate interests of the state. His attachment to equity is not motivated by some pursuit of higher standards of justice; instead, Isocratean equity wants to find a way—a creative, even unprecedented way—to seek "advantage" for the "affairs in which we act as citizens." His redefinition of equity as a tool of adroit politicking raises central questions about its role in society. Is equity a subversive principle that prompts us to critique our persistent injustices? Or is it instead a principle that equips entrenched actors to skirt criticism in the name of "reasonable" expedience? Are these two ideas—both termed *epieikeia* in the fourth century BCE—worthy of the English translation *equity*? And if so, is our own notion of equity, so often understood as a tool of radical reform, just as well understood as a vehicle for conservative continuity?

Corrupting the Youth and Reactionary Equity

When the comedian Aristophanes first staged his play *The Clouds* in 423 BCE, it was a bust. He complains about this dramatic failure in a revised version of the play, which survives today. About halfway through this later version, the leader of the chorus steps forward and berates the audience: "I took you for intelligent theatergoers and this for the most sophisticated of my comedies."[26] The plot of this "sophisticated" drama is, indeed, a bit highbrow. It centers around a father-and-son duo named Strepsiades and Pheidippides, who are desperate to escape their crushing debts and who turn to the vanguard teachings of Socrates to help them argue out of their obligations. Poking fun at the speculative endeavors of the poindexters at the city's *phrontisterion*, or "Thinkery," Aristophanes's *Clouds* shows us Socrates measuring the feet of fleas, "walking on air, and attacking the mystery of the sun."[27]

Although it garnered only a lukewarm reception at the time, the play today stands as an invaluable document about attitudes toward education in the fifth century and especially toward Socrates. It sketches a version of Socrates rather different from the inquisitive gadfly we find in Plato's dialogues. In *The Clouds*, Socrates is an unabashed radical, asking his students if they "want to learn for yourself the real, plain truth about religion" and "to talk face to face with *our* divinities, the Clouds."[28] Later in the play, he teaches Pheidippides to beat his father mercilessly. Strepsiades ultimately seeks revenge on Socrates for corrupting his son, and he summons a mob of indignant Athenians to burn down the *phrontisterion*. While the philosopher roasts alive in his school, Strepsiades calls out—joyously, vengefully—"Chase them, stone them, hit them, for all their crimes! Remember, they wronged the gods!"[29]

The violent conclusion of *The Clouds* would prove to be a prelude. Only twenty-four years after Aristophanes's play was staged, a jury of Athenians found Socrates guilty of "corrupting the youth" and "inventing new gods," sentencing him to death by hemlock. At least according to Socrates's defense that he makes for himself in Plato's *Apology*, Aristophanes's play was partly to blame for the charges brought against him: "You have seen this yourself in the comedy of Aristophanes, a Socrates swinging about there, saying he was walking on air and talking a lot of other nonsense about things of which I know nothing at all."[30] These denials were fruitless. Aristophanes's caricature of Socrates was convincing enough to assign to him a fatal punishment not entirely unlike the one he suffers at the conclusion of the play.

Socrates, of course, was not wholly an invention of Aristophanes's imagination. At least in part, the portrayal of Socrates in *The Clouds* builds on some prevailing ideas about him. (The veracity of Plato's characterization of Socrates is also a topic of scholarly disagreement.) Socrates had a "long-standing reputation as a subversive sophist," and he was "widely perceived to be a *misodemos*, an 'enemy of the people,' a perception drawn from the careers of his associates and his reputed teachings."[31] Perhaps most infamous of Socrates's students was Alcibiades, the aristocratic Athenian who was in large part responsible for his city's disastrous miscalculations during the Peloponnesian War. Especially in light of this history, Socrates was seen as an opponent of the state's dominant interests, certainly not as the state's champion.

In the years to come, however, "the trial and execution of Socrates had gained for the Academy a genuine and widely acknowledged hero and martyr."[32] Isocrates himself would capitalize on this posthumous reputation. By the time Isocrates was eighty-two years old—when he wrote his *Antidosis*—Socrates had become, for many, an intellectual model. Despite Isocrates's critiques of "hairsplitting" philosophers, in fact, he decides in that work to cast himself as, "like Socrates, ... a persecuted intellectual, ill-understood by his fellow citizens who fail to grasp the great good that he in fact accomplished for the *polis*."[33] In keeping with his opportunistic bent, Isocrates was happy to portray himself as a new Socrates at a time when such a characterization would advance his own interests.

Even if Isocrates presents himself in the *Antidosis* as a "persecuted intellectual," we should not take him for an unwelcome critic of Athenian politics and society, as Socrates had been understood earlier. In fact, scholars regularly consider Isocrates to be a spokesman for the Athenian elite, even in this very work. In her commentary on the *Antidosis*, Yun Lee Too finds in him "a conservative ideology that verges on oligarchy."[34] Takis Poulakos calls him "far more conservative than the Sophists" because he "placed his faith on the conventions of the community and took for granted the truth value of the language of the community's traditions."[35] What, in the eyes of these scholars, is so "conservative" about Isocrates's mission here? And in what ways does he show us how *epieikeia*—the same word that would become Aristotelian *legal equity*—might also be understood as a traditionalist principle?

Key to Isocrates's vision of a conservative *epieikeia* is his obsession with reputation and even political fame. As we uncovered in the preceding section, Isocrates's goal is not a high-minded pursuit of justice. In the *Encomium of Helen*, he underscores how his educational program is instead rooted in "the affairs in which we act as citizens"—his students are supposed to benefit the city-state in their practical, rather than speculative, doings. Building on this pragmatic orientation in the *Antidosis*, he frames his curriculum as one suitable for a "philosophical and ambitious" (*philosophos kai philotimos*) man—the latter word combines the prefix *philo*, meaning "lover of," and *timē*, meaning "honor."[36] Earlier we saw how Isocrates's *philosophia* encourages a practical work ethic, and his word *philotimos* builds on that very orientation. For Isocrates, there is no division between the philosopher and the reputation-seeker: his ideal philosopher is one who garners the adulation of his city by pursuing celebrated achievements.

This desire for civic celebrity provides a clearer picture of the brand of equity, or reasonableness, that Isocrates wishes to cultivate. In the *Antidosis*, he again explains how *epieikeia* itself can be a measure of political success: a promising student should "devote even more attention to ensuring that he achieves a most 'reasonable' (*epieikeitatos*) reputation among his fellow citizens. Who could fail to know that speeches seem truer when spoken by those of good name than by the disreputable?"[37] In contrast to the relentless truth-seeking practices of Socrates in the *Apology*, Isocrates seeks popular approval. An Athenian should pursue the halo of *epieikeia* since it makes his political speech "seem truer" and makes his name more influential in the public sphere. The aim of philosophical wisdom, the pursuit of ideal justice, the contemplation of divine blessedness—these high-minded goals are only peripherally relevant to the ambitious, honor-loving statesman.[38] Through this focus on *timē*, then, Isocrates presents a notion of *epieikeia* that is socially cautious and beholden to preexisting attitudes. His "reasonableness" is grounded in the confidence that others, too, would take his attitudes to be reasonable and therefore would approve of them.

Isocrates's calculated and calculating *epieikeia* resurrects some unresolved problems from Aristotle's *Nicomachean Ethics*. How do we know when to bend the rules? How much should we bend them? On whose behalf should those rules be bent at all? Isocrates's ideal philosopher—wise but also renowned—is the politician who seems reasonable and fair to the fellow citizens whose approval he craves. His "equity," then, is simply shorthand for their shared ethical expectations. Seen in this light, an Isocratean curriculum centered around *epieikeia* is one centered around the general activities, attitudes, and beliefs entrenched in a society. His "reasonableness" defers to what is already seen as commonsensical. If Socrates would come to be seen as the "enemy of the people," Isocrates wants to be seen as their efficient but obsequious servant.[39]

Millennia later, this opposition between these two philosophical thinkers and their respective educational programs comes to the fore in the mordant criticism of H. L. Mencken. People, he observes,

> seem to believe that [education's] aim is to fill the pupil's head with a mass of provocative and conflicting ideas, to arouse his curiosity to incandescence and inspire him to inquiry and speculation—in the common phrase, to teach him how to think. But this is surely nonsense. If education really had any such aim its inevitable effect would be to reduce nine-tenths of its victims to insanity, and to convert most of the rest into anarchists. What it seeks to do is something quite different—something, in fact, almost the opposite. It is financed by the state and by private philanthropies, not to make lunatics and anarchists, but to make good citizens—in other words, to make citizens who are as nearly like all other citizens as possible. Its ideal is not a boy or a girl full of novel ideas but one full of lawful and correct ideas—not one who thinks, but one who believes. If it actually graduated hordes of Platos and Nietzsches it would be closed by the Department of Justice, and quite properly.[40]

Mencken here presents figures like Plato (and, in turn, his mouthpiece Socrates) as subversive intellectuals, those whom the state would view as a threat to its established values and practices. Seen as a contrast to such learned agitators is the student whose training shelters him from "provocative" ideas and incisive "inquiry." Such a student substitutes provocation with "lawful and correct ideas" that uphold what the state already seeks to uphold. Known for his caustic and unapologetic pen, Mencken provides an uncomfortably cynical view of democratic education; cynical as it may be, however, his view presents a view of pedagogy that echoes Isocrates's appeals to convention. Education should make "good citizens," not inquisitive philosophers. Students should not seek out "hairsplitting" truths but generally correct "belief," or *doxa*. Perhaps students should not emerge from the schoolhouse as exact replicas, but they should be "as nearly like all other citizens as possible"—certainly within some "reasonable" range of acceptable graduates.

The Flourishing, Equitable Student

Over two thousand years after the time of Isocrates, our politics still places equity at the center of its educational aspirations. We need to look no further than the US Department of Education, which recently published its own "2022 Agency Equity Plan related to Executive Order 13985."[41] This "Equity Plan" reports that its mission "is to promote student achievement and preparation for global competitiveness by fostering educational excellence and ensuring equal access."[42] On the same page, the plan says that "to fulfill this mission, the agency must embed equity throughout its operations and mission to meet the needs of every learner." A quick search of recent scholarly literature and policy whitepapers will reveal similar language in dozens of documents. The first page of this 2022 Agency Equity Plan, however, is an especially powerful example of the protean life that equity currently enjoys in contemporary discussions of education, flitting not just between the notions of normalizing equity and "exceptional equity" that we laid out in the previous chapter but even resuscitating the state-supporting notion of *epieikeia* that we find throughout Isocrates's writings.

In the spirit of exceptional equity, this plan asks us to "meet the needs of every learner," those idiosyncratic demands of individual psychology and even physical ability.[43] We hear echoes of normalizing equity in the report's calls to "address longstanding disparities in college access" as well as "underlying systemic barriers—those policies and practices that have been drivers of inequitable outcomes" among racial, geographic, and socioeconomic groups.[44] In addition to these threads of normalizing and exceptional equity, moreover, the 2022 Agency Equity Plan parallels Isocratean notions of the civic benefits of "reasonable" priorities enshrined in *epieikeia*: the principle of pursuing practical outcomes on behalf of the larger political community, here hinted at under the banner of "global competitiveness." We should, according to both Isocrates and the Department of Education, set aside "hairsplitting" and set our minds to the pressing problems of the day.

The Department of Education—that is, an arm of the state itself—is not the only institution that sees equity through such a pragmatic, Isocratean lens. The RAND Corporation's researchers similarly define educational equity around these practical outcomes: "Educational equity is fair and just access to the support and resources necessary to achieve a student's full academic and social potential." Students are educated not simply in the service of their intellectual growth but also for their (and society's) utility. Echoing the Agency Equity Plan above, RAND also returns to the normalizing and exceptional brands of equity, underscoring how an equity-based curriculum should "teach students with disabilities" and confront "the education challenges that immigrants and refugees face."[45] We should pursue fairness for the particular hurdles of a student with disabilities and for the children of underserved ZIP codes. At the level of lexicography, then, policy papers show us over and over how we simply do not have one consistent idea of this "essentially contested concept," particularly when we consider matters of the classroom.

In the previous chapter, I proposed a separation of two species of equity—equity of the exception and equity of the norm—both of which try to advance justice but in opposite ways. This brief investigation of Isocrates and his echoes in contemporary discussions of educational equity have introduced another dimension of this idea's complex intellectual history. As his *epieikeia*-centered agenda shows us, sometimes this very concept can be deployed not in the service of justice per se but instead in the service of practical, political objectives. For Isocrates, ideas are reasonable when they comport with society's activities and aims. This second dimension of equity exposes the tension between values we set for ourselves as individuals and values demanded by our social lives. The question at hand is not so much "toward what 'reasonable' standard of justice do we strive?" but instead "who gets to determine these 'reasonable' standards, and how are they determined?"[46]

As with exceptional and normalizing equity, this second aspect of *epieikeia* has a long history, one we see in Isocrates and even in his archrival, Plato. In the first books of the *Republic*, Socrates famously positions justice not just as an attribute of the individual person but also as a virtue of the city as a whole.[47] Isocrates makes a similar maneuver when he presents equity as both a matter of individual training and one of civic prosperity. The political theorist and classicist Danielle Allen perhaps has this ancient doubling in mind when she writes in her book *Education and Equality* that modern education should strive for two goals, one centered around social utility and the other around individual enrichment. Drawing on thinkers ranging from Aristotle to Hannah Arendt, she observes first that a "state asserts authority over education as a matter of securing social reproduction."[48] By echoing a softer version of Mencken's state education that attempts to "make citizens who are as nearly like all other citizens as possible," Allen recognizes—like Plato and Aristotle and Isocrates—that the state uses education to advance its own interests.

But over and above these state-centric goals, Allen also sketches a second (but not inferior) function of education, which is fundamentally "eudaemonistic," leveraging Aristotle's vocabulary of *eudaimonia*—"happiness," "blessedness," or "flourishing." Not to be confused with a form of utilitarianism that seeks to produce the "greatest good," Allen's notion of educational eudaemonism designates "an ethical outlook organized around the efforts of individuals to achieve their full human flourishing by means of the development of their internal capacities."[49] An education system constructed around these pointedly "internal" aims requires that "each student must always be an end in himself, not a means to some other end" like social or economic utility.[50] In Allen's eyes, the best system of education—to paraphrase another political mind of our own era—will ask not just what we can do for our country but what our country can do for us.

Allen's explicit advocacy for eudaemonism gives us a distinct version of the two-pronged program of education we find in Isocrates: his produces careerist politicians, hers "flourishing" persons. The difference is especially sharp when we return to Isocrates's candid aspiration for honor (*timē*) and the "most reasonable (*epieikotatos*)" reputation. Although both Isocrates and Allen acknowledge the state's valid educational interests, Isocrates doggedly focuses on "the affairs in which we act as citizens," rejecting the "useless" even in our personal educational projects. But for Allen, education need not help us achieve a respected title even when it keeps one eye on "political empowerment." Allen sees an ideal of education in activities like reading novels and other domains of the literary arts, for she contends, "If verbal empowerment is at the base of political empowerment and if the humanities have a special impact there, then we have a case for the humanities."[51] By reorienting individual training around such empowerment rather than naked political clout, Allen recasts the Isocratean program as one that redefines the aims of civic education. The student gets to express their own views of politics. They do not merely get ahead by the rules and standards of "reasonableness" already set for them.

In that sense, Allen's view of education is one refracted through a democratic lens: values are not simply pressed on us by the state, but we participate in their creation and revision. Surprisingly, we might also take inspiration from Isocrates himself on this front. While he defers to prevailing ideas of honor and reasonableness, he nevertheless acknowledges that these values are subject to change and reimagination. In *Against the Sophists*, Isocrates again trains his sights on Plato and other philosophers on these very questions. There, he disapproves of how they "fail to notice that they are using an ordered art (*tetagmenē technē*) as a model for a creative activity (*poiētikon pragma*)."[52] Isocrates's claim here demands our careful attention to the distinction in Greek between a so-called *technē* (an "art" or a "skill") and *poiēsis* (something composed creatively or artistically). A *technē*, from which English gets its words *technical* and *technique*, denotes a systematic body of knowledge that—on account of its orderliness—can be taught clearly to another. We might think of computer programming as a kind of *technē* since mastery of such a topic involves the technical grasp of a firm, stable collection of rules and principles.[53]

Isocrates refuses to think of justice, politics, and equity in these "technical" terms. His brand of civic-minded training is instead a "creative activity," a *poiētikon pragma*. Words like *poiētikon* or *poiēsis* ("creation," "production") or *poiētēs* ("poet," "maker") all grow out of the Greek verb *poiein*, meaning "to make" or "to produce." The Isocratean project, then, revolves around creative faculties rather than some scientific or systematic knowledge. We do not memorize the formulas of political success; we instead craft them. We do not calculate the equal treatment of citizens; we instead construct it. We do not repeat the same, steady slogans in a changing society, but we attend to "circumstances (*kairoi*), propriety (*to prepon*), and originality." In Isocrates's view, to put it briefly, other Athenian intellectuals consider matters like equity and justice something we "know." For him, it is something that we "make"—or at least something that *some* people make.

This claim that politics or justice is something we construct rather than know might sound like a maxim of deconstructive, postmodern philosophy, but it can be found in all sorts of classically oriented thinkers. In the pursuit of political equality, Danielle Allen urges educators to develop the internal capacities of their students rather than have them memorize moral laws. In his reading of Aristotle, Myles Burnyeat insists that we learn to be good by fostering a "general evaluative attitude" through practice and incremental growth.[54] In his account of American juries and their role in fostering the "practice" of equity among Americans, too, Tocqueville notes how jury deliberation "is incredibly useful in shaping the people's judgment and augmenting their natural enlightenment. . . . It should be seen as a free school."[55] These philosophers—like so many earlier thinkers—follow in Aristotle's footsteps by positioning ethical learning, including matters like equity, as the product of experience rather than of a long night in the library. Justice is something we hone through practice, not something we acquire from a page. In an Isocratean vein, they see our understanding of justice as a "creative activity," and we ourselves are the product.

This tradition that we find in Isocrates, Aristotle, Tocqueville, and others is an intellectual antecedent to the anti-idealist vision in Richard Rorty, whom we encountered in the previous chapter as an ally of equity of the exception. In urging us to see opportunities to revise our ever-shifting ideas of "human solidarity," he recommends that we abandon the transcendental philosophy of Plato and turn instead to "ethnography, the journalist's report, the comic book, the docudrama, and, especially, the novel."[56] Like Allen, he sees these narratives as tools for personal "empowerment" and developing of our "internal capacities," not just books to display on the shelf or even to consult for firm doctrine. In a way, Rorty resuscitates the sophistic debates of the fourth century, where Isocrates similarly rejected the project of teaching ethical knowledge as though it were an "ordered art" like geometry or logic. Anticipating Rorty's "turn against theory and toward narrative," Isocrates centers "creative activity" as a method of building our capacity for equity. We do not learn what equity is by being given a definition or even a set of rules. Perhaps Rorty, if he were alive today to witness our ongoing cultural fascination with equity, would recommend that we set aside instructive works like Ibram Kendi's *How to Be an Antiracist* and instead watch *The Wire* or read *Bleak House*, the narrative building blocks of our own equitable attitudes.

These "builders" of equity—as opposed to its "finders"—draw us back to the second dimension of equity I sketched a few pages ago. *Epieikeia*, or equity, might be a kind of "reasonableness," but reasonable according to whom? We may wish to instill ethical values through the docudrama, but which docudrama? We may see equity as a tool of humanistic, political empowerment, but empowerment of whom, and empowerment toward what end? Perhaps a citizen should direct their efforts toward the "important matters" of their society, but important for what reason?

The answers to these kinds of questions are never obvious. Often writers do not even attempt to answer them. When Aristotle in the *Nicomachean Ethics* urges the equitable person to bend the law, he tells us neither how far to bend it nor for precisely what reasons. Cicero, too, says the ideal constitution includes a "certain *aequabilitas*," but he never maps out its contours. Perhaps these ambiguities are unavoidable: the consistent quality of equity seems to be its resistance to "near formulation in rules or traditional precepts," as Burnyeat puts it. (Even the Court of Chancery, building on its decisions and compiling a system of equitable precedent alongside common law, seems to have understood that equity could not be straightforwardly defined.) In his old age, Isocrates may have positioned himself—*contra* Plato—as the founder of these later intellectual traditions. Even if we bristle at his naked careerism and deference to state-approved priorities, he still contends that people have a role in refining, ever refining, their vision of a fair, reasonable, equitable society. He simply gave the state—rather than all its citizens—the most authority for defining its values.

I bring this chapter to a close with a provocation, rooted in Isocrates's comments about this "creative" approach to justice and equity. What none of the above authors suggests is that equity is a matter of stringent rule-following and bureaucratic fealty. I imagine they would see administrative "equity policies" as a contradiction in terms: *epieikeia* and *aequitas* have never been concise rules, nor have they been legal formulas. Pointing to the creative ambiguities surrounding equity, they would reject the imposition of rigid policy in its name. For them, equity was never a matter of compliance.

I do not intend to excuse defiance and contrarianism, nor do I invite a kind of nihilism that rejects equity's existence in the first place. But I do want to extend an invitation for readers to give some thought, grounded in these multifarious histories, about whether we see equity as an "attitude" of fairness that we cultivate instead of a rule that we learn from a list of best practices. To return to one of Danielle Allen's intellectual inspirations, Hannah Arendt exhibits a suspicion across her writings of a society that "expects from each of its members a certain kind of behavior, imposing innumerable and various rules . . . to make them behave."[57] In her rejection of a society structured around such "rules," Arendt champions a political environment that allows space for the "activity" of civic life, for "no activity can become excellent if the world does not provide a proper space for its exercise."[58] Equity requires work, not just study. A book like this one was never going to give its readers a clear, simple directive on how to become equitable citizens or how to check it off our collective to-do list. No single book, in fact, ever could.

Conclusion

On May 15, 2023, Florida Governor Ron DeSantis signed into law Senate Bill 266, also known as House Bill 999. As part of its goal to "revis[e] the mission of each state university," the bill prohibits such institutions from "expend[ing] any funds, regardless of source, to promote, support, or maintain any programs or campus activities . . . that espouse diversity, equity, and inclusion or Critical Race Theory rhetoric."[1] Not just a restriction of university funding, the bill also requires state colleges and universities "to remove from [their] course catalogues any specified major or minor in critical race theory, gender studies, or intersectionality or any derivative major of these belief systems."[2] Months before the bill passed, the American Council of Learned Societies called it a "frontal attack" on academic freedom, predicting "dire consequences for . . . teaching, research, and financial well-being" at Florida's institutions of higher learning.[3] The warning proved prophetic. As the *New York Times* reported in December of the same year, the University of Florida saw that among its faculty, the rate of "overall turnover [went] from 7 percent in 2021 to 9.3 percent in 2023," with a 30 percent turnover rate at its law school.[4]

Over and above these attacks on faculty independence, Senate Bill 266 also makes it impossible to discuss several foundational texts and questions in the Western philosophical tradition. Indeed, demonstrating the durable presence of equity in that very tradition has been one central aim of the preceding chapters. An earnest prohibition of "campus activities" that "espouse diversity, equity, and inclusion" would forbid reading groups on Aristotle's *Nicomachean Ethics*, lectures on the historical understanding of judicial power as specified in the US Constitution, and coursework on Greco-Roman views of civic education. Restricting discussion of "intersectionality" would turn teaching Cicero's *De Re Publica* and its implications for modern "proportional equality" or *aequitas* into a high-wire act of self-censorship. It would be similarly impossible to teach John Stuart Mill's *On Liberty*, Alexis de Tocqueville's *Democracy in America*, and of course, Charles Darwin's *The Descent of Man* without some investigation of diversity.

Viewed against the backdrop of these banned topics and texts, the bill proves to be bitterly ironic. While it perhaps inadvertently restricts discussion of Thomistic law and Ciceronian politics, it simultaneously empowers the Board of Trustees of the University of Florida to "establish and fund the Hamilton College for Classical and Civic Education," whose purpose is "to support teaching and research concerning the ideas, traditions, and texts that form the foundations of Western and American Civilization."[5] Specifically, this new college would "educate university students in core texts and great debates of Western civilization and the Great Books."[6] Insofar as a "Great Books" curriculum includes Aristotle, Cicero, and the authors of the *Federalist Papers*, Senate Bill 266 demands that its universities' professors design courses around texts and topics—among them, equity—that it simultaneously forbids. The bill, in short, is self-refuting.

Certainly, Senate Bill 266's proponents will argue that it is not Aristotle's equity they want to ban from classrooms. It is not Cicero's book on republican constitutional design that should be struck from the curriculum. The bill's text makes that clear. Its targets are critical race theory, gender studies, and intersectionality. Only these novel, vanguard forms of equity are harmful to students, they might contend, but the historical discussions of *epieikeia* and *aequitas* that appear in the pages of this book should remain central to Florida's classrooms. Indeed, I do not imagine Florida legislators have any intention of outlawing the study of Article III of the US Constitution, nor do I think they intend to turn the fifth book of Aristotle's *Nicomachean Ethics* into campus contraband to be smuggled into dorms like philosophical Bud Light.

As this book has shown, however, such a division between ancient and modern notions of equity is impossible. Hamilton's comments on equity in the *Federalist Papers* draw from the *Nicomachean Ethics*, and those early American thinkers in turn inform our own fights over methods of statutory interpretation. Isocrates's framing of *epieikeia* as the standard of "reasonableness" amenable to state interests anticipates and stages debates about the role of subversive thought in our curricula. While the writings of Kimberlé Crenshaw, Danielle Allen, H. L. Mencken, and Myles Burnyeat are all innovative in their approaches to matters like justice, education, and equality, they did not emerge *ex nihilo*. They, like us, are building on the conceptual roots found in the inescapable thought and terminology of their predecessors.

Advancing not just an ahistorical understanding of equity, the Florida legislature has a reductive, static view of one of the richest and most protean concepts in Western ethics. By taking "equity" as shorthand for a concrete policy they don't like—say, race-conscious hiring overseen by "DEI officers"—rather than as an ethical principle worthy of debate, Senate Bill 266 shuts down discussion of difficult and contentious problems of policy and ethics. These attitudes are profoundly antithetical to academic inquiry. Matters like equity are precisely those that deserve to be treated among the bill's "great debates of Western civilization." If terms like *freedom*, *justice*, *authority*, *truth*, and *citizenship* deserve to be taught in Florida's universities, then so should *equity* (as well as *diversity* and *gender*). Indeed, all these topics appear in the texts discussed in this very book, including those earliest writings of Plato, Isocrates, and Aristotle. By excluding equity or diversity from campus curricula, Senate Bill 266 has simply designated an incuriously narrow set of ideas that Floridians are allowed to debate.

As a point of illustration, it might be helpful to turn to some of these other terms that no legislature would dream of barring from university classrooms. Concepts like freedom and justice are subject to contentious disagreement, from the ancient world to the modern. As we saw in the opening chapter of this very book, Thrasymachus offers a view of justice rooted in forcing one's will on another. And by calling this rule "freer" than obeying any moral standards, Thrasymachus similarly gives us an alternative view of "freedom" rooted in exploitation and license, a view that Socrates spends the remainder of the *Republic* countering.[7] Other terms are similarly disputed. As one of America's chief theorists for enshrining "religious tolerance" among our national values, John Locke nevertheless argues that "those are not at all to be tolerated who deny the being of God" since "promises, covenants, and oaths, which are the bonds of human society, can have no hold" over atheists.[8] Adam Smith, the godfather of modern capitalism, tells his readers that the widespread benefits of productive labor are nevertheless borne out of a "base and selfish disposition," adding a complex, moral dimension to his unplanned miracle of economic growth.[9] That equity would have a similarly complicated and sometimes paradoxical intellectual history is in keeping with the many other foundational concepts whose clear meaning eludes us, inspiring salutary and necessary coursework for these students on the cusp of full citizenship.

On this front, I want to return to Martha Minow's suggestion that equity—like many of the concepts named above—enjoys the status of being an "essentially contested concept." Earlier we may have seen this designation as a mark of philosophical failure. I take it to be the opposite. As I wrote at the conclusion of the preceding chapter, equity deserves to be treated more like a topic of academic debate rather than a matter of compliance or bureaucratic protocol. To be sure, the Florida legislature is not the only institution mistaken in this regard. In the first pages of this book, we surveyed how corporations have co-opted the language of equity to pursue their own ends, similarly confusing a philosophical subject for a business agenda. As equity becomes more the domain of human-resources departments, we see the regrettable bureaucratization of a problem properly suited to open-ended inquiry. We should not, in other words, look to policy as the domain of equity, whether in the reactionary politics of Florida's legislature or in the workplace infrastructure of the corporation.

I am not the first nor the only academic to recognize this brand of conformist anti-intellectualism. Many in our contemporary culture—critics of equity cited here but also some of its champions—are victims of what St. John's College tutor Zena Hitz calls "opinionization," which she defines as "the reduction of thinking and perception to simple slogans and prefabricated positions."[10] Hitz bemoans this phenomenon in her 2020 book *Lost in Thought*, which extols quiet moments of contemplation but catalogs how "much of what counts as education in the contemporary scene is the cultivation of correct opinions," whether the "much-maligned education supported by progressive activists, education that seeks primarily social and political results" or the "conservative mirror image of progressive activism: the promotion of correct opinions about free markets."[11] In her view, contemporary education produces sloganeering, not critical thoughtfulness.

Our own thoughtless discourse around equity today reveals how this adulterated notion of intellectualism, one "that could be boiled down to the mastery of a set of sentences," extends far beyond the lecture hall. Perennial, rich debates about the nature of justice, like the very debates that begin Plato's *Republic*, have been reduced to memes, replacing judicious consideration with mindless recitation. And Senate Bill 266's blanket prohibition against discussions of equity (or at least what it pronounces equity to be) gives this mindlessness the force of the law. Our cultural moment appears to be one in which equity has exchanged its multidimensional, paradoxical richness with a calcified, "opinionized" slogan. To present equity as a static sound bite—"equal outcomes," "a Marxist assault on the rule of law," "critical race theory"—is to remain willfully ignorant of centuries of ethical, legal, and educational thought by some of the most foundational writers in history.

Many centuries ago, in the *Nicomachean Ethics*, Aristotle urged his students to recognize that their most carefully constructed statutes would govern unpredicted futures. His lesson was one of humility—a recognition that even the most learned among us are far from omniscient. In light of these limitations, he turns to the leaden rule of the builders from Lesbos, that flexible measure for constructing homes and streets out of misshapen stone. Aristotle applied this metaphor to the law, but we would do well to apply it to the very principle it represents. Like the statutes of Aristotle's Greece, the concept of equity itself has come to apply to so many contexts and problems, many of which Aristotle himself could have never predicted. He did not envision England's Court of Chancery, nor would he have comprehended the racial frameworks underlying the Jim Crow South. This ignorance is not a mark of failure. It is a mark of human finitude.

Just as the leaden rule needs to bend around misshapen stones and just as statutes need to contort themselves around exceptional cases, so, too, must equity itself adapt to our ever-changing society. It has not and it cannot mean just one thing, for the very notion of reasonableness—like justice and freedom—is always being renegotiated by those who are empowered to do so. And in a functioning democratic society, citizens ought to hold that power of negotiation. To treat equity as a jingle, to allow a legislature to strip it of its philosophical complexity, or to acquiesce to a definition provided by our bosses—these are ways in which we today relinquish that power. I hope this book inspires readers to stop relinquishing it and instead to seize it.

Notes

Introduction

1. Freeman, *Alexander Hamilton*, 435.
2. Packer, "The Moral Case against Equity Language."
3. Google Trends data available at https://trends.google.com/. Accessed March 17, 2024.
4. Freeman, *Alexander Hamilton*, 171.
5. US Const. art. 3, § 2, cl. 1., https://www.archives.gov/founding-docs/constitution-transcript/.
6. Caldwell, "The Inequality of 'Equity.'"
7. Rufo, "What Critical Race Theory Is Really About."
8. Pan, "Workplace 'Anti-Racism Trainings' Aren't Helping."
9. Aleem, "REI's Union-Busting."

Chapter One

1. Plato, *Republic*, 335c. Translations of Plato's *Republic* are adapted from Cooper and Hutchinson, *Plato: Complete Works*.
2. Plato, *Republic*, 336b.
3. Plato, *Republic*, 338c.
4. Plato, *Republic*, 338d–e.
5. Plato, *Republic*, 344c.
6. Plato, *Republic*, 433a.
7. For one classic interrogation of justice itself, well beyond the scope of this book, see Rawls, *A Theory of Justice*.
8. Plato, *Republic*, 514a.

9. Plato, *Republic*, 515e–516d.
10. Plato, *Republic*, 509d.
11. Plato, *Republic*, 510a.
12. Plato, *Republic*, 511c.
13. Plato, *Republic*, 510c.
14. Plato, *Republic*, 510c.
15. Plato, *Republic*, 513b.
16. For one account of this alleged requirement to enroll in Plato's Academy, see Saffrey, "Ἀγεωμέτρητος μηδεὶς εἰσίτω," 67–87.
17. Plato, *Republic*, 505a.
18. Plato, *Republic*, 505a.
19. Plato, *Republic*, 506c.
20. Plato, *Republic*, 343b–c.
21. Plato, *Republic*, 452a. Socrates's comment here specifically refers to the proposal of radical equality between men and women in his ideal city, which was certainly a jarring idea to the ancient Athenians.
22. For Augustine's particular affinity for Platonic philosophy, see *City of God* 8.1–11.
23. Aristotle cites Plato as his philosophical predecessor by name in *Nicomachean Ethics* I.4, 1095a32, as part of his rejection of the Platonist form of the good.
24. Aristotle, *Nicomachean Ethics* I.6, 1096b22–24. Translations of Aristotle's *Nicomachean Ethics* are adapted from Broadie and Rowe, *Nicomachean Ethics*.
25. Aristotle, *Nicomachean Ethics* I.6, 1096b24–25.
26. Aristotle, *Nicomachean Ethics* I.6, 1097a9–11.
27. Aristotle, *Nicomachean Ethics* I.6, 1097a11–13.
28. Aristotle, *Nicomachean Ethics* I.3, 1094b13–17.
29. Other Platonic dialogues, however, are more amenable to the idea of "imprecision" in legal matters. On this thread of Platonic thought, see Eden, *Poetic and Legal Fiction*, 28–29.
30. Aristotle, *Nicomachean Ethics* I.3, 1094b24–28.
31. Aristotle, *Nicomachean Ethics* II.6, 1106a35–b5.
32. Aristotle, *Nicomachean Ethics* II.6, 1106b35–1107a2.
33. For an investigation of virtues as reflections of the embedded attitudes and expectations of one's cultural context, see Annas, *Intelligent Virtue*, especially chapter 4.
34. Aristotle, *Nicomachean Ethics* V.1, 1129a34.
35. Aristotle, *Politics* III.10, 1281a20–21. Translations of Aristotle's *Politics* are adapted from Reeve, *Politics*. The final sentence of *Nicomachean Ethics* (1181b23–24) announces the "start on the discussion" of constitutions, laws, and customs, often taken as a gesture toward the topics treated in *Politics*.

36 Aristotle, *Politics* III.16, 1287a28–30.
37 Aristotle, *Politics* III.16, 1287a30–32.
38 Aristotle, *Politics* III.15, 1286a8–15.
39 Wexler and Irvine, "Aristotle on the Rule of Law," 14.
40 Aristotle, *Politics* III.16, 1286a20–23.
41 Aristotle, *Nicomachean Ethics* V.10, 1137a32.
42 For standard translations of *epieikeia*, see *LSJ epieikeia*. The Aristotelian ethicist MacIntyre, *Whose Justice?*, 119, observes that the English word *equity* is used in the context of the "law to name something very like that type of exercise of legal judgment to which Aristotle is referring" in this chapter of the *Nicomachean Ethics*.
43 Aristotle, *Nicomachean Ethics* V.10, 1137b30–31.
44 Aristotle, *Nicomachean Ethics* V.10, 1137b31–32.
45 Barr, "A Rule That Bends," 154.
46 Eden, *Poetic and Legal Fiction*, 13. This image of the leaden rule, "which can be bent to fit the shape of every stone, just like the judge adapts the law to the facts of each case, was a common theme among medieval and early modern theologians when they referred to *epieikeia*" (Maniscalco, *Equity in Early*, 33). We return to this image's resurgent interest in the following chapter.
47 Herodotus, *Histories*, 3.80.
48 *Oxford English Dictionary*, s.v. "seemliness (n.)," July 2023, https://doi.org/10.1093/OED/1130673098.
49 For one consideration of *eikos*, its possible translations into English, and its complicated position in Platonic philosophy, see Burnyeat, "Εικως Μυθος," 143–165.
50 Aristotle, *Nicomachean Ethics* V.10, 1137b34–35.
51 See, for instance, Aristotle's *Topica* 141a16, where Aristotle again provides a definition of *epieikeia* as a method of statutory interpretation to be used with "strict laws." The word even extends beyond the Aristotelian corpus, and indeed, *epieikeia* is a word that predates Aristotle. In the final chapter of this book, we turn to Isocrates, whose earlier considerations of justice, education, and virtue revolve around the same term.
52 Aristotle, *Nicomachean Ethics* V.10, 1137b35–1138a4. Here, Aristotle uses the masculine adjective *epieikēs* to describe a person rather than the noun *epieikeia* to denote a broader principle.
53 Aristotle, *Nicomachean Ethics* I.1, 1094a1–2.
54 Burnyeat, "Aristotle on Learning to Be Good," 72.
55 For Aristotle's own argument on the related point that "a person is not just and moderate because he does just things but also because he does them in the way in which just and moderate people do them," see *Nicomachean Ethics* II.4, 1105b8–9.

56 The adjective *epieikes* (with a short epsilon rather than a long eta in the final syllable) is the neuter adjective, here perhaps best understood as "a reasonable thing" rather than "a reasonable person."
57 Aristotle, *Rhetoric* I.13, 1374a26–31. Translations of Aristotle's *Rhetoric* are adapted from Freese, *The "Art" of Rhetoric*.
58 Aristotle, *Rhetoric* I.13, 1374a33–34.
59 MacIntyre, *Whose Justice?*, 120.
60 Aristotle, *Rhetoric* I.17, 1374b10–22.
61 Maniscalco, *Equity in Early*, 33.

Chapter Two

1 Dawkins, *The Selfish Gene*, 206.
2 Although the comic itself is no longer available from its original publisher, its brief history can be found in Levinson, Geron, and Brighouse, "Conceptions of Educational Equity," 1–12.
3 Levinson, *et al.*, "Conceptions of Educational Equity," 2.
4 For a comprehensive account of *aequus* in Latin literature, see *TLL* vol. I 1, 1028, 64ff.
5 Varro, *On the Latin Language*, 7.23.
6 We might expect to find the Latin word *aequalitas* as the antecedent of our English word *equality*, but *aequalitas* is comparatively rare, especially among classical sources. The *TLL* reports (vol. I 1, 1002, 14ff.) just three appearances in the writings of Cicero, with many more in late antique authors like Augustine and Boethius.
7 For a consideration of the Hellenic origins of this particular example of Indian sculpture, see Stalwart, "The Provenance of the Gandhāran," 3–12.
8 Horace, *Epistles*, 2.1.156–157. The translation is my own.
9 For a rich account of Cicero's debt to Plato for this dream episode, see Coleman, "The Dream of Cicero," 1–14.
10 Plato, *Republic*, 557c.
11 For the recommendation that "philosophers rule as kings in their cities," see Plato, *Republic*, 473c–d.
12 Zetzel, *De Re Publica*, 1.52. Translations are adapted from Zetzel, *On the Commonwealth and On the Laws*.
13 Zetzel, *De Re Publica*, 1.53. As James Zetzel explains in his commentary, these statements are not made by Scipio Aemelianus, the principal interlocutor in Cicero's dialogue, but instead by some unnamed "advocate of aristocracy" (*On the Commonwealth and On the Laws*, 22).
14 Zetzel, *De Re Publica*, 143.

15 James Zetzel (*De Re Publica*, 132) sums up this critique of democratic *aequabilitas* with a "modern adaptation of the sentiment . . . 'When everybody's somebody, then no one's anybody.'"
16 Part of the confusion surrounding these terms may be deliberate in *De Re Publica*. In James Zetzel's reading, the aristocratic speaker "confuse[s] juridical equality and social equality . . . just as the democrats blur the distinction between equal rights and equal power" (*On the Commonwealth and On the Laws*, 23).
17 In his own introductory comments on Cicero's political vocabulary, James Zetzel emphasizes how "*aequitas* can only mean fairness of equity, not equality" (*On the Commonwealth and On the Laws*, xxxiv).
18 Cicero, *De Re Publica*, 1.43. Although this statement comes from Scipio Aemelianus rather than the unnamed critic of democracy who speaks at 1.53, James Zetzel notes that "the same criticism of democracy is expressed" (*De Re Publica*, 142).
19 The combination of social and legal inequality presents some interpretive problems for these passages, as suggested above in note 16.
20 Elaine Fantham, "*Aequabilitas* in Cicero's Political Theory," 287.
21 *Aequitatem dico non utique bene iudicandi . . . sed se cum certeris coaequandi, quam Cicero 'aequabilitatem' vocat* (Lactantius *Inst.* 5.14.15, see *TLL* vol. I 1, 992, 84. The translation is my own.).
22 Perhaps we might even translate *aequabilitas* here more precisely as the rare English word *equability*, which, according to the *Oxford English Dictionary* (s.v. "equability (n.)," July 2023, https://doi.org/10.1093/OED/1056646459), carries as its primary meaning "the quality of being equable or uniform; evenness of mind, temper, or behaviour; freedom from fluctuation or variation in condition, rate of movement, degree of intensity, etc." The same entry reports that its use has declined since 1800 and appears only "0.02 times per million words in modern written English."
23 Zetzel, *On the Commonwealth and On the Laws*, xxxiv.
24 Chroust and Osborn, "Aristotle's Conception of Justice," 137.
25 Aristotle, *Nicomachean Ethics*, 5.3, 1131a25–31, 1131b17–18.
26 Aristotle, *Nicomachean Ethics*, V.3, 1131a22–24.
27 Even if Cicero ascribes these views to speakers in the dialogue, readers take those views to be Cicero's own, for his "moralistic language only thinly veils the fact that Cicero is approving a constitutional device to give political power to the wealthy in proportion to their wealth—no surprise perhaps in view of his respect for property and those dignified by its ownership in actual political life" (Fantham, "*Aequabilitas* in Cicero's Political Theory," 288).

28 For a recent, extended consideration of merit and its role in structuring a society, see Sandel, *The Tyranny of Merit*.
29 Zetzel, *On the Commonwealth and On the Laws*, xxxiv.
30 Cicero, *De Re Publica*, 1.69.
31 Asmis, "A New Kind of Model," 402.
32 Polybius, *Histories* 6.10, as paraphrased by Asmis (2005, 402).
33 In her own view, Asmis writes that "what creates the equilibrium is a certain equality among individuals," preserving Cicero's ambiguity between the "equilibrium" among the constitution's political elements and the "equality" among the citizens who themselves comprise the state's population (2005, 403).
34 van Zyl, "Justice and Equity of Cicero," 173.
35 MacIntyre, *Whose Justice?*, 120.
36 van Zyl, "Justice and Equity of Cicero," 167. Fantham (1973) explains, "In less formal situations, *aequitas* denotes either the spirit of the law, as opposed to *scriptum* or *litterae*, or fair treatment" (286).
37 Cicero, *Topica*, 1.2. Translation adapted from Cicero, *On Invention*.
38 Cicero, *Lucullus*, 2.119. Translation adapted from Cicero, *On the Nature of the Gods*.
39 Cicero, *De Inventione*, 2.46. Translation adapted from Cicero, *On Invention*. For a fuller discussion of Cicero's understanding of the "accommodative power" of *aequitas* in the Latin tradition, see Eden, *Hermeneutics and the Rhetorical Tradition*, 7–19.
40 Eden, *Hermeneutics and the Rhetorical Tradition*, 15.
41 The opposition between the letter and the spirit of the law can similarly be found in Aristotle's *Rhetoric* as the conflict between *dianoia* (intention) and *logos* (word), anticipating the Latin terminology (1.13.17). On "the discrepancy between the writer's words and intention" as treated in the rhetorical tradition, see Eden, *Hermeneutics and the Rhetorical Tradition*, 11.
42 Eden, *Poetic and Legal Fiction*, 40.
43 Quintilian, *Institutio Oratoria*, 3.6.60. Translations and citations of Quintilian are adapted from Quintilian, Marcus Fabius, *The Orator's Education*.
44 Quintilian, *Institutio Oratoria*, 3.6.61.
45 See *Oxford English Dictionary*, s.v. "letter (n.1), sense II.6," March 2024, https://doi.org/10.1093/OED/8020148421.
46 Maniscalco, *Equity in Early*, 95.
47 We should not understand Maniscalco here to mean that the use of *aequitas* was rare for exploring the "fair" reconciliation of the letter and the spirit of the law. Indeed, the entry for *aequitas* in our most authoritative Latin dictionary includes over one hundred lines of examples of *aequitas* used in this very context (see *TLL* vol. I 1, 1015, 38ff.).

48 Quintilian, *Institutio Oratoria*, 7.6.7. Here Quintilian uses the adjective *aequum* rather than the abstract noun *aequitas*, but the etymological stem is the same.
49 Reinhardt, *Cicero's Topica*, 203–204.
50 Zetzel, *On the Commonwealth and On the Laws*, xxxiii. Zetzel continues, "*Ius* also has the connotation of 'justice'—that is, the broader principles of equity or morality which a legal system is supposed to embody" (xxxiv). Cicero himself explains how these principles of *iustitia* are not statutory but instead natural or perhaps even intuitive: "Justice (*iustitia*) is a habit of mind which gives every man his desert while preserving the common advantage. Its first principles proceed from nature" (*De Inventione*, 2.53.160).
51 Tacitus, *Dialogus de Oratoribus* 40.4. Translations of Tacitus's text are adapted from Hutton et al., *Agricola, Germania, Dialogue on Oratory*.
52 Here we move to the medieval period, but *aequitas* remained an important concept for theological, literary, and ethical matters in the intervening centuries. For a study on the application of *aequitas* to matters of scriptural interpretation, for instance, especially as they figure in Augustine's *De Doctrina Christiana*, see Eden, *Hermeneutics and the Rhetorical Tradition*, 41–63.
53 Maniscalco, *Equity in Early*, 23.
54 For a collection of examples of *misericordia* as it appears in the rhetorical and legal contexts of the classical period, see *TLL* vol. VIII 1124, 84ff.
55 Maniscalco, *Equity in Early*, 29.
56 See, for instance, how the Latin Vulgate uses *aequitas* at Psalms 51:5, where the Greek of the Septuagint uses *dikaiosunē*.
57 Aristotle, *Rhetoric*, I.17, 1374b10–22.
58 Van Zyl, "Justice and Equity of Cicero," 173.
59 Maniscalco, "Justice and Equity of Cicero," 34, provides Aquinas's citation in context: *epieikeia quod apud nos aequitas dicitur* (*Summa Theologiae* 2.120.1). For a Latin text of the relevant *quaestio* of the *Summa Theologica*, see https://aquinas.cc/la/en/~ST.II-II.Q120.
60 Riley, *The History, Nature*, 31.
61 Ambiguity or *ambiguitas* was a separate issue in the Hermagorean framework discussed in this chapter. For one discussion of *ambiguitas* in classical rhetorical practice, see McNamara, "The Ethics of Ambiguity in Quintilian."
62 Maniscalco, *Equity in Early*, 43.
63 Maniscalco, *Equity in Early*, 36.
64 Maniscalco, *Equity in Early*, 37.
65 Maniscalco, *Equity in Early*, 219.

Chapter Three

1. For both the Italian text and the English translation supplied here, see Alighieri, *Inferno*, 3.9.
2. Maniscalco, *Equity in Early*, 6.
3. Increasingly, however, Aristotle's writings became available for those without knowledge of ancient Greek. For a study of Aristotle's translation and reception by medieval and Renaissance thinkers, see Reffini, *The Vernacular Aristotle*.
4. For studies of Lucretius's powerful influence on early modern science and philosophy, see Greenblatt, *The Swerve*, and Palmer, *Reading Lucretius*.
5. Maniscalco, *Equity in Early*, 6.
6. For these various historical examples of "epiky" and its lexicographical variants, see *Oxford English Dictionary*, s.v. "epiky (n.)," July 2023, https://doi.org/10.1093/OED/5345163819.
7. Fortier, *The Culture of Equity*, 69.
8. Fortier, *The Culture of Equity*, 68.
9. Fortier, *The Culture of Equity*, 59.
10. Hobbes, *Leviathan*, 17.13. Citations of Hobbes's *Leviathan* are drawn from Noel Malcolm's 2012 Clarendon Press edition.
11. Hobbes, *Leviathan*, 17.13.
12. Hobbes, *Leviathan*, 13.9.
13. Hobbes, *Leviathan*, 13.9.
14. Hobbes, *Leviathan*, 17.13. In the same passage, Hobbes leaves open the possibility that the sovereign might be "one man, or one assembly of men," so his *Leviathan* is not, strictly speaking, an apologia for absolute monarchy.
15. Hobbes, *Leviathan*, 17.13.
16. Hobbes, *Leviathan*, 15.1.
17. Hobbes, *Leviathan*, 21.8.
18. In many ways, Hobbes saw his writings as a break from earlier humanist traditions, but as we see even in this brief treatment of *Leviathan*, his thinking owes much to his classical and humanist predecessors. For a robust treatment of his complicated position in this intellectual history, see Skinner, *From Humanism to Hobbes*.
19. Hobbes, *Leviathan*, 15.15.
20. Hobbes, *Leviathan*, 15.15.
21. It would, however, be incorrect to say that Hobbes innovates not at all in his thinking about distributive justice. Rather than rely on any abstract ideas about merit or desert, he provides a "pure procedural account of equity [that] is fundamentally different from the scholastic/Aristotelian notion of distributive justice" since "Hobbes leaves it to the

sovereign to determine what is due to whom" (Olsthoom, "Hobbes's Account of Distributive," 32). Like Aquinas before him, Hobbes is also indebted to Christian thought on matters of justice since, when he defines the violation of equity as προσωπoληψία (Hobbes, *Leviathan*, 15.24), he uses a "Greek term, meaning partiality towards the rich or powerful, [that] is from the New Testament" (Malcolm 2012, 237 cited in Hobbes, *Leviathan*).

22 Hobbes, *Leviathan*, 26.21.
23 Hobbes, *Leviathan*, 26.20.
24 Hobbes, *Leviathan*, 26.26.
25 Hobbes, however, seems to use a Latin vocabulary broader than just *aequitas* to capture this sense of *epieikeia* when his English resorts to *equity*. See, for instance, his translation of *equity* as *quod aequum est* at 26.26.
26 Olsthoom, "Hobbes's Account of Distributive," 18.
27 Olsthoorn, "Hobbes's Account of Distributive," 19.
28 Olsthoorn, "Hobbes's Account of Distributive," 30–31.
29 Olsthoorn, "Hobbes's Account of Distributive," 30–31.
30 Worthington, "Equity as a System of Law."
31 Worthington, "Equity as a System of Law."
32 Watt, "Earl of Oxford's Case."
33 Watt, "Earl of Oxford's Case." This citation of *mercy* as the origin of the Court of Chancery reminds us that equity was not simply taken as an inheritance from Aristotle but also drew from the notion of *misericordia* developed in the Middle Ages.
34 That is not to say that equity was a complete rejection of *stare decisis*. Almost as a parallel system of law that developed its own tradition of precedent, the Court of Chancery, after centuries of rulings, would come to rely on earlier rulings in the name of fairness. The result was that equity emerged as "an appendix and complement to the common law, and unintelligible apart from it, [that] operated [in] separate courts, adopting and applying different practices to meet the demands placed upon them" (Worthington, "Equity as a System of Law").
35 Even if the Court of Chancery no longer exists as a formal judicial body in England, its principles of equity are still studied in English law. Anglophone lawyers still grapple with the sometimes muddy relationship between law and equity, and one widely cited article on the distinction between them calls equity a "mysterious creature" (Burrows, "We Do This at Common," 1).
36 Wood, *The Creation of the American Republic*, 295.
37 Wood, *The Creation of the American Republic*, 283. Hobbes was not the only social contract theorist whose ideas would prove influential on the early Americans, and perhaps even more influential was John

Locke, whose *Second Treatise on Government* anticipates American Revolutionary sentiments when it assigns to the state the function of "preservation of [citizens'] lives, liberties, and estates" (§123).

38 Wood, *The Creation of the American Republic*, 249.
39 Wood, *The Creation of the American Republic*, 301.
40 Wood, *The Creation of the American Republic*, 301.
41 Wood, *The Creation of the American Republic*, 301.
42 Aristotle, *Rhetoric*, I.13, 1374a33–34.
43 Wood, *The Creation of the American Republic*, 303.
44 Wood, *The Creation of the American Republic*, 303.
45 Wood, *The Creation of the American Republic*, 457.
46 Wood, *The Creation of the American Republic*, 458.
47 For an extended treatment of equity's role in the revolutionary histories of England, America, and France, see Fortier, *The Culture of Equity in Restoration and Eighteenth-Century Britain and America*, 63–118.
48 Freeman, *Alexander Hamilton*, 435.
49 Compare, too, the following example from the *Oxford English Dictionary* (See *Oxford English Dictionary*, s.v. "equity (n.), sense II.4.a," December 2023, https://doi.org/10.1093/OED/2957382373) conveying a similar sense: "1853 T. I. Wharton Digest Cases Pennsylvania 708 Equity will grant relief when . . . a contract is made under a mistake."
50 There are two famous Romans by the name Brutus suggested by this choice of pseudonym. The first was Lucius Junius Brutus, one of the architects of the overthrow of Tarquin the Proud, the last of the kings of Rome. After deposing Tarquin in 509 BCE, Lucius Junius Brutus then became one of the first two consuls—the top executive position—of the incipient Roman Republic. Marcus Junius Brutus, who lived about five hundred years later, traced his family history to this founding republican figure, and he himself would embark on his own overthrow of tyranny by lending his hand to the assassination of Julius Caesar in 44 BCE. (His participation in this plot is immortalized in the dying words of Caesar, according to Shakespeare: *Et tu, Brute?*)
51 Bailyn, *The Debate on the Constitution*, 2:131.
52 Bailyn, *The Debate on the Constitution*, 2:132.
53 Bailyn, *The Debate on the Constitution*, 2:133.
54 Bailyn, *The Debate on the Constitution*, 2:175.
55 Even if these arguments parrot Aristotle's own reasoning in the *Nicomachean Ethics*, the pseudonymous author cites Hugo Grotius, not Aristotle, as his source for this theory of equity (Bailyn, *The Debate on the Constitution*, 2:132).

56 Waldstreicher, *John Quincy Adams*, 203.
57 For one recent study of the influence of Greco-Roman antiquity on the intellectual culture of the early Americans, see Ricks, *First Principles*.
58 Bailyn, *The Debate on the Constitution*, 1:408.
59 Bailyn, *The Debate on the Constitution*, 1:409.
60 Wood, *The Radicalism of the American Revolution*, 235.
61 For his part, Wood, *The Radicalism of the American Revolution*, nevertheless maintains that "the Revolution . . . made America into the most liberal, democratic, and modern nation in the world" (7).
62 Tocqueville, *Democracy in America*, 316.
63 Tocqueville, *Democracy in America*, 316.
64 Burnyeat, "Aristotle on Learning to Be Good," 72.
65 Tocqueville, *Democracy in America*, 337.
66 Tocqueville, *Democracy in America*, 293.

Chapter Four

1 *Rationale of Judicial Evidence*, from Bowring, *7 Works*, 291.
2 This rejection of legal flexibility seems to soften over the course of Plato's writings. Later Platonic texts—particularly Plato's *Laws*—embrace *epieikeia* as a remedy for inflexible statutes, anticipating some elements of Aristotle's account in the *Nicomachean Ethics*. For one account of Plato's embrace of legal imprecision, see Eden, *Poetic and Legal Fiction*, 28–32.
3 For Bentham's rejection of natural rights as "nonsense upon stilts," see Bentham, *Rights, Representation, and Reform*, 317–375.
4 Bentham, *The Works of Jeremy Bentham*, 292. In a footnote on the preceding page, Bentham continues, "England had once its court of star-chamber: . . . Explain the business of a court of equity by a definition of equity? As well might explain the business of the star-chamber by the definition of a star." In the same work, he seems to draw little if any distinction between equity and equality: "Equity is, in its original signification, exactly synonymous to its conjugate equality" (295).
5 Rufo, "What Critical Race Theory Is Really About."
6 Rufo, "What Critical Race Theory Is Really About."
7 Garner, *Garner's Modern English Usage*, 218.
8 Garner, *Garner's Modern English Usage*, 218.
9 Virgil, *Aeneid*, 6.309. Translations of the *Aeneid* are adapted from Virgil. *Eclogues. Georgeics. Aeneid, Books 1–6.* Translated by H. R. Fairclough. Revised by G. P. Goold. Cambridge, MA: Harvard

University Press, 1999. *Quam multa in silvis autumni frigore primo / lapsa cadunt folia, aut ad terram gurgite ab alto / quam multae glomerantur aves, ubi frigidus annus / trans pontum fugat et terris immittit apricis* (trans. Fairclough and Goold, 1999).

10 *Altae moenia Romae*, 1.7. Careful readers of the Latin will observe that Virgil transfers the adjective *altae* to Rome itself, but other modern translators, including Fairclough and Goold (used here), Robert Fagles, and Robert Fitzgerald nonetheless write "high walls" rather than "high Rome."
11 Minow, "Equality vs. Equity," 173.
12 Minow, "Equality vs. Equity," 188. Minow further underscores that "the terms are often used for overlapping or interchangeable meanings." For a foundational treatment of "essentially contested concepts," see Gallie, *Philosophy and the Historical Understanding*, especially chapter 8.
13 Wexler and Irvine, "Aristotle on the Rule of Law," 14.
14 For one recent example of "an equity perspective of fairness in assessment," see Tai et al., "How Are Examinations Inclusive," 390–402.
15 Like educational assessment, views on equity in sentencing vary "depending on one's philosophy" but take into consideration "the severity of the crime, the defendant's prior criminal history, or characterological considerations" (Stanfiel, "Criminal Justice Decisionmaking," 37). The same article clarifies that "it is not mere uniformity in sentencing which should be the goal but rather a fair and rational approach which allows for variability."
16 Minow, "Equality vs. Equity," 173.
17 For the etymological links among *providentia, prudentia*, and *phronēsis*, all of which were recognized in antiquity, see *TLL* vol. X 2, 2377, 21ff.
18 Minow, "Equality vs. Equity," 176.
19 Minow, "Equality vs. Equity," 176.
20 Minow, "Equality vs. Equity," 177.
21 Minow, "Equality vs. Equity," 176.
22 Plato, *Republic*, 434b–c.
23 Crenshaw, "Demarginalizing the Intersection," 139.
24 Crenshaw, "Demarginalizing the Intersection," 140.
25 Crenshaw, "Demarginalizing the Intersection," 141. For the case at the center of her analysis here, see *DeGraffenreid v. General Motors Assembly Division*, St. Louis, 558 F.2d 480 (8th Cir. 1977).
26 Crenshaw, "Demarginalizing the Intersection," 143.
27 "Kimberlé Crenshaw on Intersectionality."
28 Aristotle, *Nicomachean Ethics* I.3, 1094b13–17.

29 Murray, *Collected Essays and Memoirs*, 59.
30 Sappho, 16.1–4 (Carson, *If Not, Winter*, 27).
31 Contrary to Sappho's narrative here, other ancient sources frame Helen's story as her seizure by the Trojans rather than her willing departure. Consider, for instance, the account of her "rape" (*harp-agē*) in Herodotus's *Histories* 1.3.2.
32 Sigmund Freud, "Civilization and Its Discontents," in *The Freud Reader*, ed. Peter Gay, 768.
33 For the inspiration of this terminological shift and an account of how Aristotelian "equity accommodates each individual case, negotiating between the universality of the law and the randomness of particular circumstance," see Eden, *Poetic and Legal Fiction*, 44.
34 For Rorty's view of Freud's "return to the particular," see especially Rorty, *Contingency, Irony, and Solidarity*, 30–39.
35 Rorty, *Contingency, Irony, and Solidarity*, 192.
36 Rorty, *Contingency, Irony, and Solidarity*, 192.
37 Rorty, *Contingency, Irony, and Solidarity*, 196.
38 Rorty, *Contingency, Irony, and Solidarity*, xvi. In a more colorful phrasing of a similar idea, Rorty explains how he wants us, like Freud, to refrain from "relegat[ing] the vast majority of humanity to the status of dying animals" (*Contingency, Irony, and Solidarity*, 35).
39 Rorty, *Contingency, Irony, and Solidarity*, xvi.

Chapter Five

1 Hamilton, *The Greek Way*, 253.
2 Thucydides, *The History of the Peloponnesian War*, 2.37. Translations of Thucydides are drawn from Thucydides, *The Landmark Thucydides*.
3 Hamilton, *The Greek Way*, 258.
4 Thucydides, *The History of the Peloponnesian War*, 2.51.
5 Poulakos, "Rhetoric and Civic Education," 75. Depew and Poulakos, Introduction to *Isocrates and Civic Education*, argue that Plato and Isocrates were "wary competitors, conceding important points to each other precisely in order to distinguish themselves and their pedagogical wares from the other" (10–11). Others such as Konstan, "Isocrates' 'Republic,'" and Morgan, "The Education of Athens," have taken a more measured approach in positioning Plato and Isocrates as intellectual opposites.
6 Isocrates, *Antidosis*, 269. Translations of Isocrates's *Antidosis* are adapted from Mirhady and Too, *Isocrates I*.

7 As Hariman, "Civic Education, Classical Imitation," 226, summarizes Isocrates's desperate circumstances, he "lived through the period in which Athens suffered military defeat and occupation, the loss of empire, tyranny and retaliation within the city, the breakdown of civic values, economic exploitation, and social turbulence."
8 Homer, *Iliad*, 9.443. Translation is my own.
9 Isocrates, *Against the Sophists*, 21. Translations of *Against the Sophists* are adapted from Mirhady and Too, *Isocrates I*. The question would prove perennial for Greek philosophers, and "the question 'Can virtue be taught?' is perhaps the oldest question in moral philosophy" (Burnyeat, "Aristotle on Learning," 69).
10 Isocrates, *Against the Sophists*, 21.
11 Isocrates, *Against the Sophists*, 21. Here Isocrates denies that his teaching is merely training for "speechmaking," hinting at the longstanding opposition between "real" philosophy and rhetoric, the practice of persuasion. The validity of this opposition—and philosophy's need for persuasive language—would pervade classical thought among both the Greeks and the Romans, and it remained a perennial problem even for early modern reformers like Francis Bacon and Thomas Hobbes.
12 Isocrates, *Antidosis*, 270. If we take Isocrates's claim that he wrote the work at the age of eighty-two, placing the composition of the *Antidosis* at about 354 BCE, he is likely to have written this text about twenty or so years before Aristotle penned his own ethical treatises, including the *Nicomachean Ethics*.
13 Isocrates, *Antidosis*, 271.
14 Isocrates, *Against the Sophists*, 12–13.
15 See the entry for καιρός in Diggle, *The Cambridge Greek Lexicon*, definitions 3 and 6.
16 Roman writers would often translate the Greek word *prepon* as *aptum*—that which is "apt" or "appropriate" or "fitting." In the standard reference work on ancient rhetorical terminology, the principle of the *prepon* refers to "the relationship of the whole speech and its components to the social circumstances of the speech" (Lausberg, *Handbuch der Literarischen Rhetorik*, §1057).
17 Isocrates, *Encomium of Helen*, 4–5. Translations of the *Encomium of Helen* are adapted from Mirhady and Too, *Isocrates I*.
18 Aristotle, *Nicomachean Ethics* I.3, 1094b24–28. Even if "the dating of this speech has proved problematic," classicists agree that Isocrates's *Encomium of Helen* was composed sometime between 390 and 370, still about half a century before the composition of the *Nicomachean Ethics* (Mirhady and Too, *Isocrates I*, 32).
19 Depew, "The Inscription of Isocrates," 158.

20 Aristotle, *Nicomachean Ethics* V.10, 1137b34–1138a2.
21 Burnyeat, "Aristotle on Learning to Be Good," 72.
22 Aristotle, *Nicomachean Ethics* X.8, 1178b22–25.
23 Depew, "The Inscription of Isocrates," 173.
24 Aristotle, *Nicomachean Ethics* V.10, 1137b24–25.
25 According to the reading of Depew, "The Inscription of Isocrates," 173, the "blurring of the distinction between cleneverness and [practical wisdom] in Isocrates' *Antidosis* provides a plausible explanation of why Aristotle goes out of his way to say [. . . that] a clever man may be bad (*kakos*), while a practically wise man is by definition good, even though on occasion he can, and must, be clever as well."
26 Aristophanes, *Clouds*, 520–522. Translations of *The Clouds* are adapted from Henderson, *Aristophanes*.
27 Aristophanes, *Clouds*, 225.
28 Aristophanes, *Clouds*, 250–253.
29 Aristophanes, *Clouds*, 1506–1509.
30 Plato, *Apology*, 19c. Translations of Plato's *Apology* are adapted from Cooper and Hutchinson, *Plato: Complete Works*.
31 Villa, *Socratic Citizenship*, 13.
32 Ober, "I, Socrates . . .," 27.
33 Ober, "I, Socrates . . .," 37.
34 Too, *A Commentary on Isocrates' Antidosis*, 25.
35 Poulakos, "Rhetoric and Civic Education," 61. Hariman, "Civic Education, Classical Imitation," 226, underscores that Isocrates understood this cultural nostalgia to be a doomed project: "If temperamentally conservative, he also knew that the past golden age could not be reborn—indeed, that it had been one cause of the subsequent troubles."
36 Isocrates, *Antidosis*, 277. Careful readers of Plato will recognize that the soldier class in the ideal city is composed of those who are "honor-loving," whereas the philosopher kings are "wisdom-loving" (or "philosophical"), setting a clear distinction between these two qualities. For Plato's description of a *timocracy* of honor-loving politicians as an adulteration of his utopia ruled by true philosophers, see Plato, *Republic*, 548a–550b.
37 Isocrates, *Antidosis*, 278.
38 A similar sentiment appears earlier in the *Antidosis* when Isocrates frames "intellect," or *phronēsis*, as a cognitive capacity whereby we can "make everything more valuable" and "help each other to achieve *epieikeia*" (212).
39 The interpretation of ancient Greek virtue more generally as a matter of conservative cultural values has been explored elsewhere. For one discussion of the argument that virtues "will owe so much to the

40 Mencken, *Prejudices*, 509.
41 "2022 Agency Equity Plan."
42 "2022 Agency Equity Plan," 1.
43 For an example of such "exceptional equity" in contemporary education literature, see Tomlinson, *The Differentiated Classroom*.
44 "2022 Agency Equity Plan," 8.
45 "Educational Equity."
46 For one treatment of these fundamental questions, especially as treated by ancient authors and their readers, see MacIntyre, *Whose Justice?*.
47 See, for instance, Socrates's claim in Book 2 that "a just man won't differ at all from a just city with respect to the form of justice but will be like it" (435a).
48 Allen, *Education and Equality*, 12.
49 Allen, *Education and Equality*, 11.
50 Allen, *Education and Equality*, 11.
51 Allen, *Education and Equality*, 48.
52 Isocrates, *Against the Sophists*, 12.
53 Perhaps, however, mathematicians would reject such a firm division, which would preclude notions of "elegance," "beauty," or "creativity" from proofs and algorithms.
54 Burnyeat, "Aristotle on Learning to Be Good," 72.
55 Tocqueville, *Democracy in America*, 316.
56 Rorty, *Contingency, Irony, and Solidarity*, xvi.
57 Arendt, *Human Condition*, 40. For Arendt's accusation that the "ideological thinking [of ordering] facts into absolutely logical procedure [. . . and proceeding] with a consistency that exists nowhere in the realm of reality" leads to totalitarianism, see Arendt, *Origins of Totalitarianism*, 471.
58 Arendt, *Human Condition*, 49.

Conclusion

1 Florida Senate Bill 266, lines 3–4, 272–275.
2 Florida Senate Bill 266, lines 175–177.
3 "The Effort to Undermine Academic Freedom."
4 Saul, "In Florida's Hot Political Climate."
5 Florida Senate Bill 266, lines 289–294.
6 Florida Senate Bill 266, lines 296–297.
7 Plato, *Republic*, 344c.

(Note 39 continued) social and cultural contexts within which we have learned them that they will be effectively trapped within those contexts," see Annas, *Intelligent Virtue*, 53.

8 Locke, *Political Writings*, 426.
9 Smith, *The Wealth of Nations*, 380. Smith's remark here comes as a secondary conclusion of his chapter titled "Of the Accumulation of Capital, or Of Productive and Productive Labour" (II.iii).
10 Hitz, *Lost in Thought*, 167. I had the good fortune to read Hitz's *Lost in Thought* for *Commonweal* ("Minds Stocked Only with Opinions," September 2020), and I am grateful to Hitz for her useful vocabulary for diagnosing these intellectual ills.
11 Hitz, *Lost in Thought*, 193.

Bibliography

Aleem, Zeeshan. "REI's Union-Busting Podcast Shows How Diversity Programs Can Be Abused." *MSNBC*, February 11, 2022. https://www.msnbc.com/opinion/msnbc-opinion/rei-s-union-busting-podcast-shows-how-diversity-programs-can-n1288965.

Alighieri, Dante. *The Divine Comedy 1: Inferno*. Translated by John D. Sinclair. New York: Oxford University Press, 1961.

Allen, Danielle. *Education and Equality*. Chicago: University of Chicago Press, 2016.

Arendt, Hannah. *The Human Condition*. Chicago: University of Chicago Press, 1998.

———. *The Origins of Totalitarianism*. New York: Harcourt, 1973.

Asmis, Elizabeth. "A New Kind of Model: Cicero's Roman Constitution in De Republica." *American Journal of Philology* 126, no. 3 (2005): 377–416.

———. "The State as a Partnership: Cicero's Definition of *Res Publica* in His Work *On the State*." *History of Political Thought* 25, no. 4 (2004): 569–599.

Augustine. *City of God*. Introduction by G. R. Evans. Translated by Henry Bettenson. London: Penguin Books, 2003.

Bailyn, Bernard, ed. *The Debate on the Constitution*. 2 vols. New York: Library of America, 1993.

Barr, Timothy. "A Rule That Bends: Aristotle on Pathos and Equity." *Philosophy and Rhetoric* 54, no. 2 (2021): 149–170.

Bentham, Jeremy. *Rights, Representation, and Reform: "Nonsense upon Stilts" and Other Writings on the French Revolution*. Edited by Philip Schofield, Catherine Pease-Watkin, and Cyprian P. Blamires. *The Collected Works of Jeremy Bentham*. Oxford: Clarendon University Press, 2002.

———. *The Works of Jeremy Bentham*. Edited by John Bowring. London: UCL Press, 1843.

Bowring, John, ed., *7 Works*. London: UCL Press, 1843.

Broadie, S., and C. Rowe, eds. and trans. *Nicomachean Ethics*. Oxford: Oxford University Press, 2002.

Burnyeat, Myles. "Aristotle on Learning to Be Good." In *Essay's on Aristotle's Ethics*, edited by A. Rorty, 69–92. Berkeley: University of California Press, 1980.

———. "Εικως Μυθος." *Rhizai* 2, no. 2 (2005): 143–165.

Burrows, Andrew. "We Do This at Common Law but That in Equity." *Oxford Journal of Legal Studies* 22, no. 1 (2002): 1–16.

Caldwell, Christopher. "The Inequality of 'Equity.'" *National Review*, April 29, 2021. https://www.nationalreview.com/magazine/2021/05/17/inequality-of-equity/.

Carson, Anne. *If Not, Winter: Fragments of Sappho*. New York: Vintage, 2002.

Chroust, Anton-Hermann, and David L. Osborn. "Aristotle's Conception of Justice." *Notre Dame Law* 17, no. 2 (1942): 129–143.

Cicero, Marcus Tullius. *On Invention. The Best Kind of Orator. Topics.* Translated by H. M. Hubbell. Cambridge, MA: Harvard University Press, 1949.

———. *On the Nature of the Gods. Academics.* Translated by H. Rackham. Cambridge, MA: Harvard University Press, 1933.

Coleman, R. "The Dream of Cicero." *Proceedings of the Cambridge Philological Society* 190, no. 10 (1964): 1–14.

Cooper, John M., and Douglas S. Hutchinson, eds. *Plato: Complete Works*. Indianapolis, IN: Hackett, 1997.

Crenshaw, Kimberlé W. "Demarginalizing the Intersection of Race and Sex: A Black Feminist Critique of Antidiscrimination Doctrine, Feminist Theory and Antiracist Politics." *The University of Chicago Legal Forum* 139:139–167.

Dawkins, R. *The Selfish Gene*. Oxford: Oxford University Press, 1976.

Depew, David. "The Inscription of Isocrates into Aristotle's Practical Philosophy." In *Isocrates and Civic Education*, edited by David Depew and Takis Poulakos, 157–185. Austin: University of Texas Press, 2004.

Depew, David, and Takis Poulakos. "Introduction." In *Isocrates and Civic Education*, edited by David Depew and Takis Poulakos, 1–18. Austin: University of Texas Press, 2004.

Diggle, James. *The Cambridge Greek Lexicon*. Cambridge: Cambridge University Press, 2021.

Eden, Kathy. *Hermeneutics and the Rhetorical Tradition*. New Haven, CT: Yale University Press, 1997.

———. *Poetic and Legal Fiction in the Aristotelian Tradition*. Princeton, NJ: Princeton University Press, 1986.

"Educational Equity." https://www.rand.org/topics/educational-equity.html. Accessed February 24, 2024.

"The Effort to Undermine Academic Freedom in Florida House Bill 999." American Council of Learned Societies. https://www.acls.org/news/the

-effort-to-undermine-academic-freedom-in-florida-house-bill-999/. Accessed February 26, 2024.

Fairclough, H. R., and G. P. Goold. *Virgil: Eclogues, Georgics, Aeneid Books 1–6*. Cambridge, MA: Harvard University Press, 1916.

Fantham, Elaine. "*Aequabilitas* in Cicero's Political Theory, and the Greek Tradition of Proportional Justice." *Classical Quarterly* 23, no. 2 (1973): 285–290.

Florida Senate Bill 266. Act Effective July 1, 2023. https://www.flsenate.gov/Session/Bill/2023/266/BillText/Filed/PDF.

Fortier, Mark. *The Culture of Equity in Early Modern England*. London: Routledge, 2005.

———. *The Culture of Equity in Restoration and Eighteenth-Century Britain and America*. London: Routledge, 2016.

Freeman, Joanne B. ed. *Alexander Hamilton: Writings*. New York: Library of America, 2001.

Freese, J. H., ed. and trans. *The "Art" of Rhetoric*. Cambridge, MA: Harvard University Press, 1939.

Freud, Sigmund. *The Freud Reader*. Edited by Peter Gay. New York: W. W. Norton, 1989.

Gallie, W. B. *Philosophy and the Historical Understanding*. London: Chatto & Windus, 1964.

Garner, Bryan A. *Garner's Modern English Usage*. Oxford: Oxford University Press, 2009.

Greenblatt, Stephen. *The Swerve: How the World Became Modern*. New York: W. W. Norton, 2011.

Hamilton, Edith. *The Greek Way*. New York: W. W. Norton, 2010.

Hariman, Robert. "Civic Education, Classical Imitation, and Democratic Polity." In *Isocrates and Civic Education*, edited by David Depew and Takis Poulakos, 217–234. Austin: University of Texas Press, 2004.

Henderson, J., ed. and trans. *Aristophanes: Clouds, Wasps, Peace*. Cambridge, MA: Harvard University Press, 1998.

Herodotus. *The Landmark Herodotus: The Histories*. Edited by Robert B. Strassler. Translated by Andrea L. Purvis. Introduction by Rosalind Thomas. New York: Anchor Books, 2009.

Hitz, Zena. *Lost in Thought: The Hidden Pleasures of an Intellectual Life*. Princeton, NJ: Princeton University Press, 2020.

Hobbes, Thomas. *Leviathan*. Edited by Noel Malcolm. Oxford: Clarendon Press, 2012.

"Kimberlé Crenshaw on Intersectionality, More than Two Decades Later." June 8, 2017. https://www.law.columbia.edu/news/archive/kimberle-crenshaw-intersectionality-more-two-decades-later.

Konstan, David. "Isocrates' 'Republic.'" In *Isocrates and Civic Education*, edited by David Depew and Takis Poulakos, 107–124. Austin: University of Texas Press, 2004.

Lausberg, Heinrich. *Handbuch der Literarischen Rhetorik.* Stuttgart: Franz Steiner Verlag, 2008.

Levinson, Meira, Tatiana Geron, and Harry Brighouse. "Conceptions of Educational Equity." *AERA Open* 8 (2022): 1–12.

Liddell, H. G., R. Scott, and H. S. Jones, eds. *A Greek English Lexicon (LSJ).* Oxford: Oxford University Press, 1940.

Locke, John. *Political Writings.* Edited by David Wootton. New York: Mentor, 1993.

MacIntyre, Alasdair. *Whose Justice? Which Rationality?* Notre Dame, IN: Notre Dame University Press, 1988.

Maniscalco, Lorenzo. *Equity in Early Modern Legal Scholarship.* Leiden: Brill, 2020.

McNamara, C. "The Ethics of Ambiguity in Quintilian." In *Quasi Labor Intus: Ambiguity in the Latin Language,* edited by Michael Fontaine, Charles J. McNamara, and William Michael Short, 205–223. Gowanus: Paideia Institute for Humanistic Study, 2018.

Mencken, H. L. *Prejudices: Fourth, Fifth, and Sixth Series.* Edited by Marion Elizabeth Rodgers. New York: Library of America, 2010.

Minow, Martha. "Equality vs. Equity." *American Journal of Law and Equality* 1 (2021): 167–193.

Mirhady, David C., and Yun Lee Too, trans. *Isocrates I.* Austin: University of Texas Press, 2013.

Morgan, Kathryn. "The Education of Athens: Politics and Rhetoric in Isocrates and Plato." In *Isocrates and Civic Education,* edited by David Depew and Takis Poulakos, 125–154. Austin: University of Texas Press, 2004.

Murray, Albert. *Collected Essays and Memoirs.* Edited by Henry Louis Gates Jr. and Paul Devlin. New York: Library of America, 2016.

Ober, Joseph. "I, Socrates . . . The Performative Audacity of Isocrates' *Antidosis.*" In *Isocrates and Civic Education,* edited by David Depew and Takis Poulakos, 21–43. Austin: University of Texas Press, 2004.

Olsthoom, J. "Hobbes's Account of Distributive Justice as Equity." *British Journal for the History of Philosophy* 21, no. 1 (2013): 13–33.

Packer, George. "The Moral Case against Equity Language." *Atlantic,* April 2023. https://www.theatlantic.com/magazine/archive/2023/04/equity-language-guides-sierra-club-banned-words/673085/.

Pan, J. C. "Workplace 'Anti-Racism Trainings' Aren't Helping." *Jacobin,* September 2020. https://jacobin.com/2020/09/workplace-anti-racism-trainings-trump-corporate-america.

Palmer, Ada. *Reading Lucretius in the Renaissance.* Cambridge: Harvard University Press, 2014.

Poulakos, Takis. "Rhetoric and Civic Education: From the Sophists to Isocrates." In *Isocrates and Civic Education,* edited by David Depew and Takis Poulakos, 69–83. Austin: University of Texas Press, 2004.

Quintilian, Marcus Fabius. *The Orator's Education*. Vol. II. Translated by D. A. Russell. Cambridge, MA: Harvard University Press, 2002.

Rawls, John. *A Theory of Justice: Revised Edition*. Cambridge, MA: Harvard University Press, 2020.

Reeve, C. D. C., ed. and trans. *Politics*. Indianapolis, IN: Hackett, 1998.

Reffini, Eugenio. *The Vernacular Aristotle: Translation as Reception in Medieval and Renaissance Italy*. Cambridge: Cambridge University Press, 2020.

Reinhardt, Tobias, ed. *Cicero's Topica: Edited with an Introduction, Translation, and Commentary*. Oxford: Oxford University Press, 2006.

Ricks, Thomas. *First Principles*. New York: Harper, 2020.

Riley, L. Joseph. *The History, Nature, and Use of Epikeia in Moral Theology*. Washington, DC: Catholic University of America Press, 1948.

Rorty, Richard. *Contingency, Irony, and Solidarity*. Cambridge: Cambridge University Press, 1989.

Rufo, Christopher. "What Critical Race Theory Is Really About." Manhattan Institute, May 6, 2021. https://manhattan.institute/article/what-critical-race-theory-is-really-about.

Saffrey, Henri-Dominique. "Ἀγεωμέτρητος μηδεὶς εἰσίτω. Une Inscription Légendaire." *Revue des Études Grecques* 81, no. 384 (1968): 67–87.

Sandel, Michael J. *The Tyranny of Merit: What's Become of the Common Good?* London: Allen Lane, 2020.

Saul, Stephanie. "In Florida's Hot Political Climate, Some Faculty Have Had Enough." *New York Times*, December 4, 2023. https://www.nytimes.com/2023/12/03/us/florida-professors-education-desantis.html.

Skinner, Quentin. *From Humanism to Hobbes: Studies in Rhetoric and Politics*. Cambridge: Cambridge University Press, 2018.

Smith, Adam. *The Wealth of Nations*. Edited by Edwin Cannan. New York: Modern Library, 2000.

Stalwart, P. "The Provenance of the Gandhāran 'Trojan Horse' Relief in the British Museum." *Arts Asiatiques* 71 (2016): 3–12.

Stanfiel, James D. "Criminal Justice Decisionmaking: Discretion vs. Equity." *Fed. Probation* 47 (1983): 36–41.

Tacitus. *Agricola. Germania. Dialogue on Oratory*. Translated by M. Hutton, W. Peterson. Revised by R. M. Ogilvie, E. H. Warmington, and Michael Winterbottom. Cambridge, MA: Harvard University Press, 1914.

Tai, Joanna, Paige Mahoney, Rola Ajjawi, Margaret Bearman, Joanne Dargusch, Mary Dracup, and Lois Harris. "How Are Examinations Inclusive for Students with Disabilities in Higher Education? A Sociomaterial Analysis." *Assessment and Evaluation in Higher Education* 48, no. 3 (2023): 390–402.

Thesaurus Linguae Latinae (TLL). Berlin (formerly Leipzig): De Gruyter (formerly Teubner), 1900–.

Thucydides. *The Landmark Thucydides*. Edited by Robert B. Strassler. Introduction by Victor Davis Hanson. New York: Free Press, 2008.

Tocqueville, Alexis de. *Democracy in America*. Edited by Olivier Zunz. Translated by Arthur Goldhammer. New York: Library of America, 2004.

Tomlinson, Carol Ann. *The Differentiated Classroom: Responding to the Needs of All Learners*. Alexandria, VA: ASCD, 2014.

Too, Yun Lee. *A Commentary on Isocrates' Antidosis*. Oxford: Oxford University Press, 2008.

"2022 Agency Equity Plan related to Executive Order 13985." https://www2.ed.gov/documents/equity/2022-equity-plan.pdf. Accessed February 26, 2024.

van Zyl, D. H. "Justice and Equity of Cicero." *Journal for Contemporary Roman-Dutch Law* 52, no. 2 (1987): 154–174.

Varro, Marcus Terentius. *On the Latin Language*. Vol. 1. Translated by Roland G. Kent. Cambridge, MA: Harvard University Press, 1967.

Villa, Dana. *Socratic Citizenship*. Princeton, NJ: Princeton University Press, 2001.

Waldstreicher, David, ed. *John Quincy Adams: Diaries 1821–1848*. New York: Library of America, 2017.

Watt, Gary. "Earl of Oxford's Case." In *The New Oxford Companion to Law*. Edited by Peter Cane and Joanne Conaghan. Oxford: Oxford University Press, 2008. https://www-oxfordreference-com.ezp2.lib.umn.edu/view/10.1093/acref/9780199290543.001.0001/acref-9780199290543-e-701.

Wexler, Steve, and Andrew Irvine. "Aristotle on the Rule of Law." *Polis: The Journal for Ancient Greek and Roman Political Thought* 23, no. 1 (2006): 116–138.

Wood, Gordon S. *The Creation of the American Republic, 1776–1787*. Chapel Hill: UNC Press Books, 1998.

———. *The Radicalism of the American Revolution*. New York: Vintage, 1991.

Worthington, Sarah. "Equity as a System of Law." In *The New Oxford Companion to Law*. Edited by Peter Cane and Joanne Conaghan. Oxford: Oxford University Press, 2008. https://www-oxfordreference-com.ezp2.lib.umn.edu/view/10.1093/acref/9780199290543.001.0001/acref-9780199290543-e-798.

Zetzel, James E. G., ed. *De Re Publica: Selections*. Cambridge: Cambridge University Press, 1995.

Zetzel, James E. G., ed. and trans. *On the Commonwealth and On the Laws*. Cambridge: Cambridge University Press, 2017.

Index

Adams, John Quincy, 86, 88
aequabilitas, 60, 87, 96–97, 136, 151n15, 151n22; as constitutional balance, 54–55; as political equality, 47–53
aequitas, 4–5, 38, 45, 61, 65, 69, 75, 96–98, 137, 140–41, 151n17, 152n36, 152n39, 152nn47–48, 152n52, 152n56, 152n59, 155n25; etymology of, 41–42; as general ethical principle, 55–56, 62; as merit, 48–52, 152n28; as principle of statutory interpretation, 57–60, 62, 64; as proportional equality, 52–54, 72; as translation of *epieikeia*, 44, 48, 63–66
Aeschylus, 28
Against the Sophists (Isocrates), 118, 120
akribeia (precision), 22–23, 25, 27–28, 74, 108, 122, 148n29, 157n2
Alcaeus, 43
Alcibiades, 126
Aleem, Zeeshan, 3
Alexander the Great, 43, 116
Allegory of the Cave (Plato), 12–13
Allen, Danielle, 132–33, 135, 137, 141
American Council of Learned Societies, 139
Annas, Julia, 148n33, 161–62n39
Antidosis (Isocrates), 119, 126–28, 160n12, 161n25, 161n38
Anti-Federalist, 84
Apology (Plato), 28, 119, 125
Aquinas, Thomas, 61, 63–65, 68, 96, 154–55n21
Arendt, Hannah, 132, 137, 162n57
aristocracy, 5, 24, 32, 38, 45–54, 60, 86–89, 96, 100, 103, 126, 150n13, 151n16
Aristophanes, 28, 124–26
Aristotle, 6, 27–42, 47–48, 51–59, 62–63, 66–68, 71, 73, 75, 79–80, 85–86, 93, 96, 98–99, 102, 105, 108, 111–12, 117, 119, 128, 132, 135–36, 140–42, 144, 149n51, 149n55, 152n41, 154n3, 152n33, 156n55; compared to Isocrates, 120, 122–24, 128, 160n12,

INDEX

Aristotle (*continued*)
   160n18, 161n25; compared to Plato, 4, 19–26, 148n23, 157n2
Asmis, Elizabeth, 54, 152n33
Athens, 9, 19, 70, 115–17, 160n7
Augustine of Hippo, 19, 148n22, 150n6, 153n52
Augustus, Emperor, 46, 61

Bentham, Jeremy, 91–93, 97, 124, 157nn3–4
Bible, 65–66, 76, 153n56
Bleak House (Charles Dickens), 136
Boccaccio, Giovanni, 66
Boethius, 150n6
Bracciolini, Poggio, 66
Brutus (Anti-Federalist author), 84–85, 91, 156n50
Brutus 11, 84, 92
Brutus 12, 85
Burnyeat, Myles, 35, 88, 135–36, 141

Caesar, Julius, 5, 45–47, 61, 69, 156n50
Caldwell, Christopher, 2
Catiline, 47
Catullus, 109
Charles I, King of England, 69
Charles II, King of England, 69
Cicero, 5, 45, 47–59, 62–63, 65, 68–69, 71–72, 84, 86–87, 93–94, 96, 98–100, 102, 136, 140, 150n6, 150n9, 150n13, 151n17, 151n27, 152n33, 152n39, 153n50
Clouds, The (Aristophanes), 124–26
Coke, Edward, 76
common law, 75–77, 83, 155n34
conscience, 75–77, 82–84, 86
contronym, 95–97

Court of Chancery, Delaware, 77
Court of Chancery, England, 75–77
courts of equity, 5, 64, 75, 78, 83, 92, 158n4
courts of law, 4, 36, 61, 75, 77, 83
Covid-19, 1
Crenshaw, Kimberlé, 103–7, 141
Cromwell, Oliver, 69

Darwin, Charles, 140
democracy, 5, 10, 13, 20, 32, 38, 54–55, 70, 86–90, 103, 107, 116, 123, 129, 133, 145, 151n18, 157n61; aligned with *aequabilitas*, 47–53, 60, 96, 151nn15–16
Democritus, 19
De Re Publica (Cicero), 45, 47–56, 69, 87, 96, 98, 100, 102, 140, 151n16, 151n18
DeSantis, Ron, 139
Dickens, Charles, 112
diversity, 1, 3, 21, 24, 48, 106–7, 111–12, 139–42
divided line, 13–17, 19, 23–24, 26, 91, 119–20
doxa (opinion, belief), 119–20, 129
Drayton, William Henry, 78
Duane, James, 80

Earl of Oxford case of 1615, 75–77, 82–83
Ecclesiastical Leases Act 1571, 76
Eden, Kathy, 57, 159n33
education, 6, 23–24, 37, 40, 57, 86, 89–90, 101, 112–13, 117–19, 121–22, 125, 127, 129–33, 135, 140–41, 143, 149n51, 158n15
Elizabeth I, Queen of England, 76
Ellesmere, Lord, 5, 76, 83, 124

Encomium of Helen (Isocrates), 121, 127, 160n18
Epicurus, 19
epieikeia, 4–6, 30, 32–37, 40, 42, 44, 48–49, 56–60, 62–64, 66–68, 73, 96, 113, 136–37, 149n42, 149nn51–52, 153n59, 155n25, 157n2; as a disposition, 34–37; in early modern English, 66–68; etymology of, 32–34; as equity of the exception, 98; in Isocrates, 117, 119–24, 127–28, 130–32, 141, 161n38
equality, 3–5, 13, 20, 37–38, 44–49, 54–55, 60, 68, 87, 92, 101, 103, 105–6, 117, 135, 141, 148n21, 151nn16–17, 151n19, 152n33; contrasted with equity, 2, 32, 39–42, 50–52, 96–97, 150n6, 157n4; proportional equality, 52–53, 93–94, 96, 98, 100, 105–60, 140
equity of the exception (*or* exceptional equity), 98–100, 108, 110–12, 120, 123, 130–32, 135, 162n43
equity of the norm (*or* normalizing equity), 98–102, 107–8, 110–11, 130–32
Erasmus, Desiderius, 66
essentially contested concept, 97, 131, 142, 158n12
eudaimonia (blessedness, flourishing), 123, 128, 132–33

Fantham, Elaine, 51
Federalist Papers, 2, 82, 84, 86, 140–41; *Federalist* 10, 86; *Federalist* 51, 82; *Federalist* 80, 2, 82; *Federalist* 84, 82
Ficino, Marsilio, 66

Florida House Bill 999 (*or* Senate Bill 266), 139–43
Floyd, George, 1
Fortier, Mark, 67–68
forms (Plato), 4, 12–13, 15–16, 18–22, 74, 121
France, Anatole, 100
freedom, 2, 89, 92, 107–8, 110, 139; as essentially contested concept, 141–42, 144
Freud, Sigmund, 110–11, 159n38
Frogs, The (Aristophanes), 28

Garner, Bryan, 94, 97
Google, 1, 93, 148n3
Gracchus, Tiberius and Gaius, 46
Grotius, Hugo, 156n55

Hake, Edward, 67
Hamilton, Alexander, 1–2, 5, 68, 81–84, 88, 93, 124
Hamilton, Edith, 115–16
Harvard University, 86, 88
Hermagoras of Temnos, 58
History of Animals (Aristotle), 123
Hitz, Zena, 143, 163n10
Hobbes, Thomas, 5, 68–75, 78, 154n14, 154n18, 154–55n21, 155n25, 155–56n37, 160n11
Homer, 44, 108–9
Horace, 43–44, 109
Hugo, Victor, 24, 26

Iliad (Homer), 108, 117
intersectionality, 94, 104–6, 139–40
Isocrates, 6, 116–24, 126–37, 141–42
isonomia (legal equality), 33, 51

Jacobin, 3
Jay, John, 2, 81

INDEX

Jerome, 65, 153n56
justice, 2–6, 9–20, 23–24, 26–30, 33, 37, 44–47, 50, 53, 56, 59–60, 62, 63–64, 69–84, 88, 90, 98–101, 103, 105, 118–19, 120, 124, 127–29, 131–32, 134–35, 137, 147n7, 153n50, 154–55n21, 162n47; as essentially contested concept, 141–42, 144; legal justice 5, 18, 28–30, 34, 36–37, 60, 66, 71, 77, 80, 82, 85, 96, 123, 149n51

kairos (opportunity), 121, 134
kallipolis, 102, 105, 117, 161n36
Kant, Immanuel, 26
Kendi, Ibram, 136

Lambarde, William, 67
Laws (Plato), 157n2
leaden rule, 31–32, 34, 64, 98, 109, 144, 149n46
legal justice. *See* justice
Lesbian rule. *See* leaden rule
letter vs. spirit of the law. *See scriptum* vs. *voluntas*
Leviathan (Thomas Hobbes), 154n18, 154–55n21, 69–70, 72–75
Locke, John, 142, 156n37
Lucretius, 66, 154n4

Machiavelli, Niccolò, 119
MacIntyre, Alasdair, 36, 149n42
Madison, James, 2, 81, 86, 88
Maguire, Angus, 39, 49, 60
Maniscalco, Lorenzo, 59, 66, 152n47
Mao Zedong, 103
Marxism, 2, 92–94, 144

mathematics, 15–17, 23–26, 37, 108, 111, 162n53
Mather, Moses, 80
Mencken, H. L., 129, 132, 142
merit. *See aequitas*
Mill, John Stuart, 140
Milo of Kroton, 24–25, 27, 30–31, 49, 79, 98, 108
Minow, Martha, 97, 99–101, 103, 142, 158n12
misericordia (mercy), 61–62, 75, 153n54, 155n33
monarchy, 29, 32, 45, 48, 50, 54, 69–70, 83, 87, 154n14, 156n50; philosopher-king, 11, 13, 47, 90, 150n11, 151n36

Murray, Albert, 106–11
Musk, Elon, 77
Myron, 116

Nicomachean Ethics (Aristotle), 20, 22, 24–25, 27–28, 30, 32–36, 42, 52–53, 56–57, 63–65, 67, 73, 79, 85, 88, 106, 112, 117, 128, 136, 140–41, 144, 148n23, 149n42, 149n55, 156n55, 157n2, 160n12, 160n18
Numa, 46

obedience, 28, 99
Octavian. *See* Augustus, Emperor
Odyssey (Homer), 108
Omni-Americans, The (Albert Murray), 106, 109
opinionization, 143
Oxford English Dictionary, 33, 67

Pan, Jennifer, 3
Parthenon, 116

Peano, Giuseppe, 15
Peloponnesian War, 42, 116, 126
Pericles, 116
Philip II of Macedon, 43, 116
philosopher-king. *See* monarchy
philosophy, 4, 6, 11–13, 18–19, 21, 26–28, 37, 44–45, 47, 57, 66, 69–73, 87, 102, 106, 125–26, 135, 139, 142–43; Isocrates's redefinition of, 118–23, 127–29, 134
phronēsis (prudence), 30, 34, 40, 55, 81, 99, 158n17, 161n38
Plato, 4–6, 9–10, 12–17, 19–28, 33, 37, 45, 47, 60, 66, 70, 74, 84, 86, 90–91, 101–2, 105–6, 111–12, 116–23, 125–26, 129, 132, 134–36, 142, 144, 148n16, 148nn22–23, 148n29, 149n49, 150n9, 157n2, 159n5, 161n36
poiēsis (creative activity), 124, 134–37, 162n53
Politics (Aristotle), 28–30, 92, 102, 111, 148n35
Polykleitos, 116
Poulakos, Takis, 127
prepon (fitting), 121, 134, 160n16
proportional equality. *See* equality
Protagoras, 118
Publius (*Federalist* author), 1, 81
Pythagoras, 85

Quintilian, 58–59, 61, 86, 153n48

race, 92, 101, 103, 105–7, 111–12, 139–41
RAND Corporation, 131
Recreational Equipment Incorporated (REI), 3

Reinhardt, Tobias, 59
relativism, 10, 27
Republic (Plato), 4–5, 9–13, 17, 19, 22, 24, 28–29, 37–38, 45, 60, 91, 101, 105, 117–18, 161n36
republicanism, 54, 69
Rhetoric (Aristotle), 35–37, 55, 79, 152n41
Rome, 38, 43–47, 61, 95, 156n50, 158n10
Romulus, 46
Rorty, Richard, 111–13, 135–36, 159n34, 159n38
Rufo, Christopher, 2, 92–93
rule of law, 29–30, 92, 120

Sallust, 44
Sappho, 43, 109–11
scriptum vs. *voluntas* (letter vs. spirit of the law), 57–60, 62, 64, 152n36, 152n41
Shakespeare, William, 83, 156n50
Smith, Adam, 142, 163n9
Socrates, 4, 9, 14, 16–19, 22, 28, 45, 119–20, 129, 142, 162n47; justice defined by, 11–13, 18, 102, 132; trial of, 125–28
sophist, 9, 118, 126–27
Sophocles, 116
Sparta, 42, 116
spirit of the law. *See scriptum* vs. *voluntas*
Stoicism, 26

Tacitus, 61
Tarquin the Proud, 46–47, 156n50
technē (craft), 134
Thrasymachus, 9–12, 16–19, 27–29, 118, 142
Thucydides, 44, 115

timē (honor, reputation), 6, 127–28, 133
Tocqueville, Alexis de, 87–90, 94, 135, 140
Too, Yun Lee, 127
Topica (Aristotle), 57, 59
Topica (Cicero), 57, 59
tyranny of the majority, 89

University of Florida, 139–40
US Constitution, 2, 55, 74, 80–85, 87–89, 92, 140–41; Article III, 5, 82, 92, 141; Seventh Amendment, 88; Sixth Amendment, 88

US Department of Education, 130–31

Varro, 42, 48
Vergil, 44, 95–96
voluntas. See scriptum vs. *voluntas*

Wire, The, 136
Wood, Gordon, 77–78, 80, 157n61

Xenophanes of Colophon, 19

Zetzel, James, 52, 150n13, 151nn15–18, 153n50